**Mel Bay Presents**

# HANDS-on
# DULCIMER

*Developing Technique Through Exercises and Studies*

## by Mike Casey

**Online Audio**

## To Access the Online Audio Go To:
### *www.melbay.com/98392BCDEB*

1 2 3 4 5 6 7 8 9 0

*Visit us on the Web at www.melbay.com — E-mail us at email@melbay.com*

# THANKS

All exercises developed by Mike Casey unless otherwise noted.

Book layout and design by Malke Rosenfeld.

Music layout and design by Janita Baker.

Many thanks to Leo Kretzner for early inspiration and permission to use his exercises; Susan Trump, Sue Carpenter, Jerry Rockwell, Lois Hornbostel, Jill Snider and Maddie MacNeil for timely encouragement and suggestions; the many students who have tried these exercises over the years, especially Ellie Vibert; Dona Benkert for providing me the first opportunity to teach a workshop specifically on technical development; Larkin Bryant Cohen for the second.

Very special thanks to Malke Rosenfeld and Janita Baker, who both worked hard on this book and helped shape it into something much more than I dreamed possible.

# TABLE OF CONTENTS

# LIST OF EXERCISES

## Two: In the Beginning...

## Three: The Right Hand

## Four: The Left Hand

## Five: Fingerpicking

## Six: Challenges for Both Hands

## Seven: Adding Strings

# CONTENTS OF THE CD

The CD that accompanies this book contains key exercises and most of the tunes found on these pages. I encourage you to use both the CD and the written music--both your ears and your eyes--in working with this material. I tried to play each exercise in a straightforward and fairly conservative way at a slow to moderate tempo. I suggest starting even slower than the tempo on the CD. With practice, some of the exercises can eventually be played faster than what you hear. But, slow is the key! Work also towards playing these in a varied manner--changing dynamic level, tempo and even rhythms for a greater challenge and to keep you engaged. Don't worry about making mistakes (you'll hear plenty of my own imperfections on the CD!). Play through them and then go back and work on the parts of the exercise that are giving you trouble.

There are 26 tracks on the CD. Some of the tracks contain several exercises but none are more than about 4 minutes in length and most are less than three.

| Track # | | Exercise/Tune # |
|---|---|---|
| 1 | Beginning Exercises--Right Hand. | Exercise 2--And a One Strum |
| | | Ex. 3--Flatpicking |
| 2 | Beginning Exercises--Left Hand | Ex. 4A and B--Left Hand Fingering |
| | | Ex. 5--Scale Exercise in D |
| | | Ex. 6--Picks and Strums |
| 3 | Strumming Patterns | Ex. 8--Eighths and Quarters |
| | | Ex. 9--Doubling Up |
| | | Ex. 10--Jig Time |
| | | Ex. 12--Changing Strum Directions |
| | | Ex. 13--Aiming the Strum |
| 4 | Flatpicking | Ex. 15A and B--Crosspicking |
| | | Ex. 16C and D--Flatpicking Patterns |
| 5 | Guide and Pivot Fingers | Ex. 21A-D |
| 6 | Scales in Rhythm | Ex. 23A--Lower Octave Scale |
| | | Ex. 24A--Scales in Threes |
| | | Ex. 24B-F |
| 7 | Scale Fragments | Ex. 25 |
| 8 | Finger Independence | Ex. 28A, F, I, K |
| | | Ex. 29--Modal Independence |
| | | Ex. 30--Modern Independence |
| 9 | Slurs | Ex. 31--Simple Hammers and Pulls |
| | | Ex. 32A--Hammers/Pulls Lower Octave |
| | | Ex. 32C and D |
| | | Ex. 33--Hammer and Pull Exercise |
| | | Ex. 35--Slides |

# ONE

## Introduction

How many times have you watched a top musician play, practice or perform and thought, "She (or he) makes it look so easy"? Most of us learning to play an instrument know it is not always easy and marvel at musicians who seem to play effortlessly. Although the spirit with which a piece of music is played can "make it look easy," the appearance of ease also has to do with the **physicalness** of playing music. We might think a master musician is completely relaxed, but complete relaxation would mean doing nothing at all! In order to **appear** relaxed and effortless the musician must have control over the muscles used (versus those not used), an excess of strength over what is required for the piece, and an economical and efficient way of using the muscles and joints needed. In other words, a master musician has well-developed and flexible technique on his or her chosen instrument.

Possessing "good technique" means having control over basic musical elements such as volume, tone, phrasing, articulation and rhythm. This control always operates in the service of conscious artistry. Our aim as musicians is first and foremost to be creative, giving artists. Technique is a means to the end of communicating through music, but not an end in itself. But, becoming a good technician on our instrument by developing flexibility, strength and control can be an important step towards true artistry.

**Grow In Your Technical Abilities**

This book is designed to help fretted dulcimer players at all levels grow in their technical abilities by developing strength, precision, control and flexibility in both the right and left hands. Acquiring a solid technical foundation provides a base upon which to build strong musicianship, enabling one to play more satisfying music regardless of style. This is not a how-to-play manual or dulcimer method book. Rather than working through the book from beginning to end, I suggest turning to sections that interest you. You will not necessarily want to tackle every exercise in the book. Pick the ones that address difficult areas in your playing. Each section progresses from easier to harder exercises. Section Two (In the Beginning…) presents basic exercises for both right and left hands to get you started. Section Six (Challenges for Both Hands) is more advanced. In between are sections focusing on the right hand, left hand, and fingerpicking that present both easy and more difficult exercises.

By offering exercises and studies designed to develop technique, I am borrowing a learning system used by classical musicians (and others) and introducing it to this folk instrument. I recognize that this approach does not work for everyone. This is not the only way to become more skilled on an instrument, and plenty of fine music is played by musicians who are less formal about these things. But, if you are stuck making the same mistakes over and over, if you hear attractive ways of playing or styles of music that you are unable to learn, or if you simply desire to become more expressive on the dulcimer, this book may be for you!

**Dive In!**     Finally, I encourage you to dive into these exercises and ideas. All musicians have short-term and long-term "projects." Although you may not be able to play a specific piece of music or execute a particular technique right now, with regular practice over time your abilities will grow. Some techniques or exercises will take a month to learn, others may take years. But, we have years – indeed, a lifetime – in which to develop our musical abilities.

# A FEW SUGGESTED GUIDELINES

*No one gets hurt!*

Hand, finger and arm size, shape and flexibility vary greatly from one person to the next. Therefore, a few of these exercises, and certain fingerings, may not be possible for some people. Don't overdo it. If it hurts to do an exercise, don't do that one. Stop before you reach the point of having pain.

*Try hard and long.*

Hands and fingers do get stronger and more flexible over time, and the soft tissue in the hands will stretch. Gradual, step-by-step practice over long periods of time will enable you to accomplish exercises and techniques that you are unable to do now.

*Try using these exercises as warm-ups.*

Just as any athlete warms up before working out, musicians need to warm up before tackling actual music. Spending ten minutes playing these exercises each day when you first pick up your dulcimer not only warms you up, but regularly develops your technique.

*Play consciously.*

Play these exercises with as much curiosity, interest and attention to detail as you can. Just going through the motions (exercising your fingers without paying attention) has limited benefit.

*Play slowly.*

The process of developing flexible technique is grounded in slow playing. Speed will come naturally from first knowing precisely what you are doing, and then relaxing.

*Repeat.*

Repeat any given exercise as many times as you think you need to. Do the exercises in whatever order makes sense to you and feel free to change, rearrange, adapt and make up your own exercises to address the specific technical difficulties you want to work with.

*Skip Around.*

You don't have to use this book in order from beginning to end. Jump in and out of the areas that interest (or trouble!) you.

*Remember that these are **technical** exercises.*

Make them **musical,** but don't confuse them with music. Apply what you learn to the music you play.

# READING THE DULCIMER TAB

*Tuning*

All exercises and tunes are in the common dulcimer tuning of D-A-D unless otherwise noted. To tune to D-A-D, first tune the lowest-pitched string of the dulcimer to the D below middle C on the piano. The middle string is then tuned to the A above this note by fretting the bass string at the fourth fret and matching the middle string to this note. The highest-pitched string (closest to the player) is then tuned an octave above the bass string. This can be achieved by fretting the middle string at the third fret and matching the highest-pitched string to this note.

Many of the exercises, especially those for the right hand, can be played in any tuning. Others can easily be adapted for the D-A-A tuning. It is the principles behind the exercises, not the tuning of the dulcimer, that is most important.

*Music and Tablature (Tab) Staff*

The staff at the top of most exercises, with the standard musical notation, is called the music staff. The staff below but connected to the music staff, containing three or four lines and numbers, is called the tab staff.

*Time Signature*

The time signature given in the music staff at the beginning of each exercise (4/4, 6/8, etc.) remains the same for each segment of the exercise unless otherwise noted. Time signatures for some of the exercises using only the tablature staff (no music staff) are given to the left of the first tab staff.

*Strings*

Each line on the tablature staff corresponds to a string on the dulcimer. The highest line of the tab staff, the line at the top, represents what is usually the lowest-pitched string on the dulcimer. This is also the string farthest from the player as the dulcimer sits on the player's lap. Throughout the book I call this string the **bass string**. The middle line on the tab staff represents the **middle string** on the dulcimer which I label, not surprisingly, the middle string. The line at the bottom of the tab staff corresponds to the string closest to the dulcimer player which, in D-A-D tuning, is the highest-pitched string on the instrument. I call this the **melody string** throughout the book. These days dulcimer melodies are played on all of the strings, though most often on this highest-pitched string. It is simply convenient, and common enough among dulcimer players, to label this the melody string.

*Notes (Fret Numbers)*

On the tab staff, numbers indicate fret numbers and are placed on top of a line that indicates which string should be fretted. For example, a "4" placed on top of the middle line of the tablature means that the fourth fret of the middle string is to be played. A "5" on the lowest line guides you to the fifth fret on the melody string. The number 6+ stands for **the 6 1/2 fret**, added to the dulcimer in the last generation between the traditional sixth and seventh frets. Most, but not all, dulcimers have a 6+ fret. The number 13+ indicates the 13 1/2 fret which is an octave higher than the 6+ fret.

*Rhythms*

The lines below the tab staff are rhythm markings and correspond to the notes in the music staff. A single vertical line represents a quarter note. Two vertical lines connected at the bottom represent two eighth notes. A double line at the bottom gives us sixteenth notes. Half and whole notes are indicated by the notes themselves below the tab staff.

3

| *Strumming and Picking Patterns* | The direction in which to strum or pick the strings is indicated on some exercises by arrows placed below or above the tab staff. An arrow pointed up towards the top of the page represents an outward strum or pick (away from the player, towards the bass string). An arrow pointed down towards the bottom of the page indicates an inward strum (towards the player and the melody string). |
|---|---|

| *Fingerings* | Because this book focuses on technical development, which often involves increasing finger strength or flexibility, many of the exercises were written with specific fingerings in mind. These fingerings are an important key to achieving successful results with some of the exercises.

**Left hand fingerings** are placed in the tab staff, using lower case letters in italics just after the fret number to which the fingering applies. The following letters are used: *t*=**thumb**, *i*=**index finger**, *m*=**middle**, *r*=**ring**, *l*=**little**.

**Right hand fingerings**, notated for some of the fingerpicking exercises, are placed below the tab staff using upper case letters below the rhythm marking. The following letters are used: **T=Thumb, I=Index, M=Middle, R=Ring**. |

| *Slurs* | Slurs, often called hammer-ons and pull-offs, are indicated in both the music and tab staffs by a semicircle connecting two notes or two numbers. In the tab staff this circle is always above the fret numbers. If numbers connected by the slur marking are going up, it is, by definition, a hammer-on. If the numbers are descending, the slur marking indicates a pull-off. Another type of slur is a slide, which is indicated by an arrow pointing towards the fret number at the end of the slide. |

| *Held Notes (Ties)* | The tab often calls for fingers to be held in place after a note is played so that the note may sustain either below or above the following musical passage. These held notes are indicated by ties, which are semicircles similar to slur markings, but are usually much longer. Slurs connect two adjacent notes; ties stretch over a beat or two or more. For example, Exercise 41, Fingerpicking Independence Exercise, has many ties but no slurs while Exercise 32 has many slurs but no ties. |

| *Variations* | Alternate ways to play a measure or two are marked by an asterisk * above the music staff. When you reach an asterisk in the music, if you wish to try the variation, skip to the end of the tune and play the alternate measure(s) given after the last measure. The variations themselves are also marked by an asterisk. |

| *Capo* | Fret numbers in tunes that use a capo are the actual fret numbers (same as no capo) since the notes themselves do not change with the presence of the capo. For example, if the capo is placed at the third fret, then fret 3 on the tab equals the capo (it feels like an open string). The next fret (fret 4) is still the fourth fret on the instrument regardless of whether the capo is there. |

# In the Beginning...

This section offers simple right and left hand exercises for players who are just starting out. In addition, for players at all levels it provides technical guidelines and suggestions that form the foundation upon which the challenging work of later sections builds. Each topic is covered in more detail in later sections.

## WARM UP STRETCHES AND POSTURE

**Stretching frees the tension in your body and encourages energy flow...**

Although these two topics are beyond the scope of this book, they are important enough to mention briefly. I strongly recommend stretching before picking up your instrument. Musicians tend to channel tension into certain parts of their bodies (depending on the instrument) often as a result of trying too hard. Stretches that loosen the neck, shoulders and torso are particularly valuable for preventing excess tension in areas that are typically problematic for musicians. They also encourage energy to flow freely from the torso through the hands and fingers. It is important to get blood running easily through these areas (especially hands and fingers) to help muscles recover from the exertion that is to follow. Madeline Bruser, in her very useful book, The Art of Practicing, presents basic warm-up stretches for musicians along with information on why and how to stretch.

Maintaining balanced posture while playing is critical to staying free of unnecessary tension, and allows the arms, hands and fingers to work efficiently from a stable base. Again, Madeline Bruser provides a detailed description of effective posture in The Art of Practicing. Most importantly, try not to hunch over your dulcimer. Keep your back and spine in a natural-feeling straight position. Hunching the shoulders forward or collapsing the spine in any way constricts the chest, leaving the heart and lungs less room to operate. Keeping shoulders back and the chest open also allows emotional energy to flow more freely and encourages direct communication with an audience or other players.

**...as does balanced posture.**

Dulcimer players seem to strum in one of two ways: They move the wrist forwards and backwards (thereby utilizing the primary movement of the wrist) while holding the tip of the pick by the thumb and tip of the index finger (sometimes including the middle finger as well.). Or, they use a guitar-type strum that utilizes a rotary movement of the wrist (using both the primary and secondary or side-to-side movement of the wrist at the same time), while holding the pick with the thumb and side of the index finger. Either style seems to work for dulcimer players, though it is useful to experiment with both while analyzing which feels stronger, looser, and gives a more pleasing tone. With any type of strum, maintaining a loose wrist is the key to good tone and solid rhythm. The major movement in strumming should come from the wrist. Strumming from the elbow or shoulder uses too many muscles and induces more tension than desirable. This also drives the pick with a fairly stiff and inflexible system behind it, resulting in poor tone.

## Exercise #1: Simple Back & Forth Strum

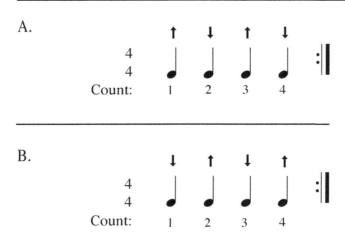

A.

B.

___

*Helpful Hints for Exercise #1*

- Dampen the strings of the dulcimer while doing the following strumming exercises by placing the left hand over the strings. Do not press down but let the hand make light contact with the strings. This will produce a click (but no actual notes since the strings will not be vibrating) when the instrument is strummed, allowing you to focus completely on the right hand and hear the strumming patterns clearly.

- Keeping the wrist loose, strum back and forth across all the strings.

# Exercise #2: Basic Dulcimer Strum ("Bum-biddy bum")

Note that this strumming pattern uses two strums in the same direction (with a short "rest" in between) followed by a strum in the opposite direction.

## A. And-A-One Strum – Starting Out

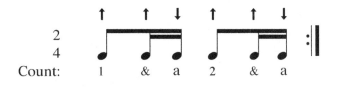

Count:    1    &  a    2    &  a

## B. And-A-One Strum – Starting In

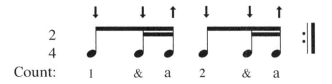

Count:    1    &  a    2    &  a

*Helpful Hints for Exercise #2*

- This is one of the basic dulcimer strums, known by a number of names including "Bum-biddy bum" and "And-a-one" strum. Dulcimer players start their strums either in (towards them) or out (away). The resulting sounds are very different: strumming in first emphasizes the highest pitched string last and can be very effective for bringing out the melody if the melody is on the string closest to the player. Strumming out first strikes the higher pitched strings first.

- Learn to strum starting in both directions so that you have more flexibility with any given piece of music.

7

# PLAYING INDIVIDUAL NOTES (FLATPICKING)

Playing one note at a time is called flatpicking. Though flatpicking is often combined with strums in actual music, it is useful to work on this technique by itself to develop the strength and precision needed to play individual notes.

## Exercise #3: Flatpicking

A. Flatpicking Fours

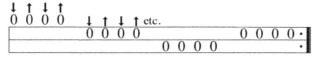

B. Flatpicking Threes

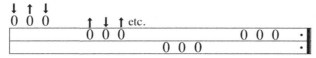

C. Flatpicking Twos

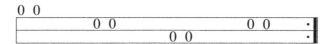

D. Flatpicking Ones

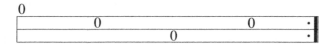

*Helpful Hints for Exercise #3*

- Alternate picking direction for each note. In 3A, pick the base string four times changing direction with the pick each time, move to the middle string and do the same thing (remembering to continue alternating direction even as you change strings), and so forth. Later we will explore flatpicking patterns that use several strokes in a row in the same direction.

- Try these exercises by picking in (towards you) on the first note but also try them by picking out on the first note.

- Repeat each exercise as often as you like. Try moving from 3A to 3B to 3C to 3D without stopping, then try mixing them up and going from one to another at random.

# THE BASICS OF LEFT HAND FINGERING

Starting now to incorporate good technique will pay huge dividends later.

Learning to use the left hand efficiently and effectively is one very big key to playing satisfying music. Starting now to incorporate the following principles of left hand fingering will pay huge dividends later when more challenging music is attempted. The following are the basic principles of left hand position and fingering, drawn in part from classical guitar technique but also common to other stringed instruments:

1.  Play on the tips of the fingers. Left hand nails need to be very short.

2.  Place fingers just to the left of frets to obtain the clearest notes. (Some compromises on the dulcimer must be made due to the long stretches required on many instruments around frets 1-3. It is often not possible to get just to the left of the fret in this area of the instrument.)

3.  Use only the minimum pressure needed for a clear note. Do not bear down onto the instrument very hard – since the instrument rests on your lap you can let gravity do some of the work for you. Keep the left hand as relaxed as possible.

4.  Keep fingers close to the instrument (do not let them lift very high away from the fretboard).

5.  Keep fingers curved. Keep the wrist curved above the fretboard (do not lock the wrist below the fretboard).

6.  Keep back fingers in place so they are ready to be used again (and don't need to be re-positioned.)

7.  Work the fingers as a unit.

One way to find a good beginning left hand position is to lay your left arm over the fretboard of the dulcimer, letting your hand and fingers dangle over the edge of the instrument. Notice the curve in your wrist and fingers. Maintaining these curves, bring your hand up and place in position on the strings. Every person's hand is different and you may need to adjust slightly to find a comfortable position.

Find a good beginning left hand position.

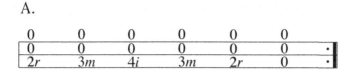

## Exercise #4: Beginning Left Hand Fingering

A.

| 0 | 0 | 0 | 0 | 0 | 0 | |
|---|---|---|---|---|---|---|
| 0 | 0 | 0 | 0 | 0 | 0 | . |
| 2r | 3m | 4i | 3m | 2r | 0 | . |

B.

| 0 | 0 | 0 | 0 | 0 | 0 | 0 | 0 | |
|---|---|---|---|---|---|---|---|---|
| 0 | 0 | 0 | 0 | 0 | 0 | 0 | 0 | . |
| 4i | 2r | 0 | 4i | 3m | 2r | 1r | 0 | . |

*Helpful Hints*
*for*
*Exercise #4*

- In 4A make sure to keep back fingers down. For example, after placing the ring finger on fret 2 and strumming, when you place the next finger down (middle finger on fret 3) leave the ring finger in place behind it. When you place the index finger on fret 4 you will have three fingers (ring, middle, index) in place on frets 2, 3, and 4 all on the same string. When it is time to come back to these fingers, they are already in place and ready to be used. This is a very efficient way to use the fingers of the left hand.

- In 4B, place the index finger on fret 4 and the ring finger on fret 2 (both on the melody string) before starting the exercise.

- In 4B when you play fret 4 for the second time, place three fingers (index, middle and ring) onto the melody string at frets 4, 3, and 2, at once as a unit before playing this part of the exercise. Then, when it is time to play frets 3 and 2 your fingers are already in position.

- Alternate strumming direction (in and out) with each strum.

## COMBINING FLATPICKING WITH LEFT HAND FINGERING BASICS

Precisely coordinating the right with the left hand is the key to solid rhythm and clear notes. Here is an exercise that will put the above flatpicking and left hand fingering skills to use while working on coordinating both hands. This exercise uses the "lower octave" of the dulcimer where the notes to the major scale are found on the bass and middle strings within the first three frets, rather than on the melody string.

# Exercise #5: Scale Exercise in D

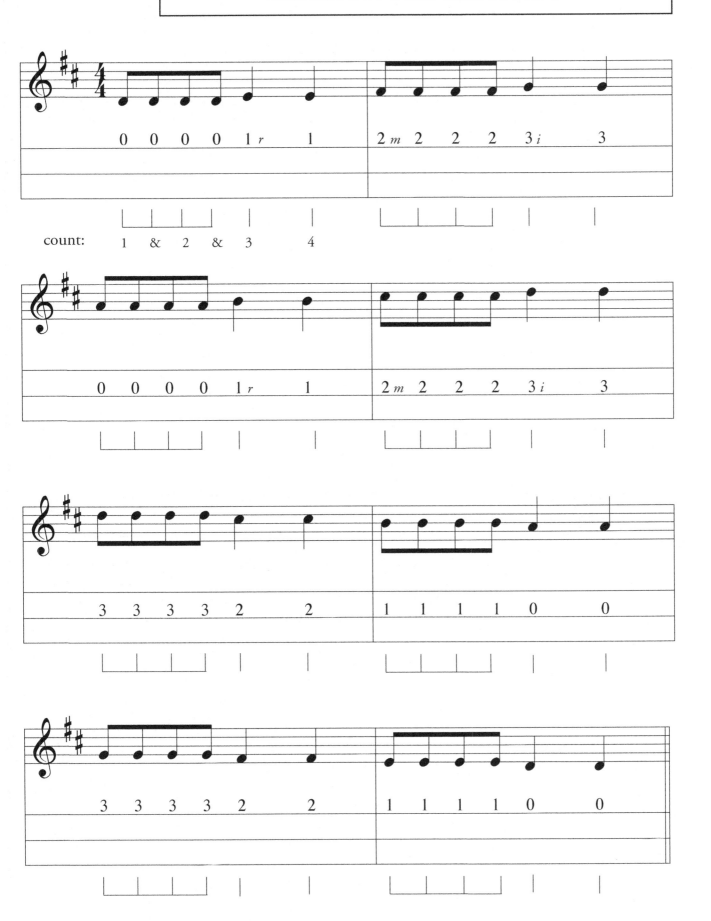

- Flatpick only the notes indicated on the bass and middle strings (do not strum all of the strings). Remember to change directions with the pick for each note (even if the note is the same as the one before).

- Start the exercise by picking in on the first note, but also try starting it by picking out.

- Follow the fingerings given in the exercise and remember to keep back fingers down. That is, when you place the index finger on fret 3 of the bass string you will also have the middle finger on fret 2 and the ring finger on fret 1 still in place.

  *NOTE: Dulcimer players with small hands or instruments with large distances between frets may have trouble keeping all of the back fingers down. One compromise is to allow the ring finger to come up when the index lands on fret 3. Another option is to finger passages like this with the thumb so that the middle finger is on fret 1, index on fret 2 and thumb on fret 3. I encourage you to try allowing your fingers to gently stretch over time so that they can reach both of these fingerings but do not hurt yourself. "No pain, no gain" does **not** apply here!*

- Work your fingers as a unit. At the beginning of measure 7, when moving from the middle string to fret 3 of the bass string, place three fingers down at once on the bass string (index on fret 3, middle on fret 2, ring on fret 1).

- For practice in keeping back fingers down, try Tune 5, Old Molly Hare.

## COMBINING FLATPICKING, STRUMMING AND LEFT HAND FINGERING BASICS

One powerful way to play the dulcimer is to alternate individual flatpicked notes with strums, taking advantage of its ability to be a self-accompanying instrument (melody and chords together). This exercise combines picking single notes with strums, done with simple left hand fingering.

# Exercise #6: Picks and Strums

- Alternate the direction of the pick stroke (whether strumming or flatpicking) with each note. The arrows at the start of the exercise will guide you.

- Remember to keep back fingers of the left hand down, just like in Exercise #4. When the index finger plays fret 4 of the melody string, the ring and middle fingers should still be in place at frets 2 and 3 of the melody string since you will be going right back to these notes.

- Tunes 1-4 in Section Eight make use of this idea of alternating flatpicked notes with chords and strums. Tune 2, The South Wind, is the easiest.

*This page has been
left blank to avoid
awkward page turns.*

# THREE

## The Right Hand

### ARTISAN or...

The right and left hands perform different functions on the dulcimer as on other stringed instruments. The difference between the two hands can be compared to the difference between an artist and an artisan. An artist is creative, generating products of the imagination. An artisan is skilled in a trade and handles the mechanics of bringing into the world what the artist creates.

In many ways the right hand is the artist, setting the strings in motion and controlling volume and tone along with much of rhythm, tempo and articulation. The right hand is creative, varying loud and soft, slower and faster, while adding emphasis and accent where desired. The left hand functions more as an artisan, preparing notes and chords to be articulated by the right hand.

### ARTIST?

We don't spend enough time working with the right hand. Too caught up with the stretching and placing of the left hand (which, admittedly, is often a challenge) we forget how much of our music depends on a strong and flexible right hand. Developing this hand goes a long way towards making our music more expressive and powerful.

## STRUMMING

Following are exercises designed to develop strength, flexibility and precision in your strumming. Remember to keep your wrist as loose and relaxed as possible through all of these exercises. Also, place your left hand lightly on the strings to get the click (no ringing strings) described on page 6.

---

### Exercise #7: Basic Dulcimer Strum with Accents[vii]

---

*Helpful Hints for Exercise #7*

■ This exercise takes the basic dulcimer strum we learned from the previous section and adds accents. Accent means emphasis or stress. A musical accent is an emphasis on a certain note, chord or beat. Accents make music rhythmically alive; practicing accents develops strength.

- Play the part to be accented a little bit harder, adding more volume than the surrounding, non-accented parts of the music.

- Play Exercise 7 first by accenting the down beat, or the beats where you count "one" and "two."

- Next, accent the upbeat or the beat where you count "and."

- For fun, try accenting the beat where you count "a."

- Try this exercise strumming in first and then again strumming out first.

## Exercise #8: Eighths and Quarters

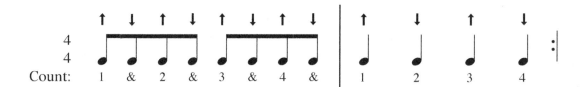

## Exercise #9: Doubling Up

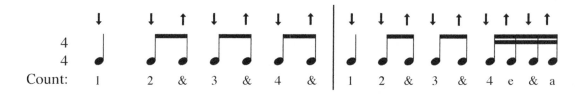

*Helpful Hints for Exercise #8 & #9*

- Try these exercises with both outward and inward strums at the beginning.

- Try accenting beats 1 and 3, then accent beats 2 & 4.

## Exercise #10: Jig Time

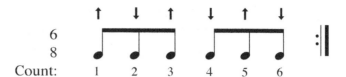

- This exercise is in 6/8 time. Try accenting downbeats (beats 1 & 4) and upbeats (beats 3 & 6).

- Try beginning the strum in both directions.

## Exercise #11: Irish Jig Strum (A) and Alternate Jig Strum (B)

A.

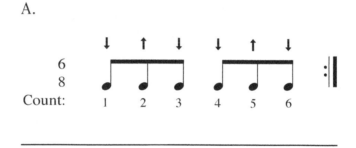

B.

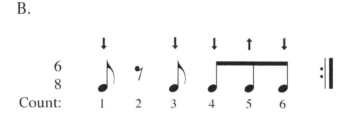

- Still in 6/8 time, but beats 3 & 4 and 6 back to 1 are strummed in the same direction. This gives a slightly more staccato feel than the jig-time strum in the previous exercise that alternates strumming direction with each beat.

- Exercise 11B simply leaves out beat 2, commonly done in Irish style accompaniment.

17

# Exercise #12: Changing Strum Directions

Count:  1  &  2  &     &  4  &  1  &  2  &     &  4  &

**Helpful Hints for Exercise #12**

- This exercise leaves silent the first half of the third beat but still maintains a change in strum direction for each note that is played. Over the course of two cycles of four beats, the direction of the strum will change for each beat. The first strum of the exercise is in, but when beat 1 comes again halfway through the strum has changed to out.

# Exercise #13: Aiming the Strum

Count:  1     2  &     3  &  4  &

**Helpful Hints for Exercise #13**

- This exercise helps develop precision by aiming the strum at some strings but not others. Using the basic pattern given above, follow this sequence.

  1. Strum just the melody string once through the basic pattern.
  2. Strum the melody and middle strings together once through the basic pattern.
  3. Strum all three strings once through the basic pattern.
  4. Back to strumming the melody and middle strings together.
  5. Back to strumming just the melody string.

- Try the exercise again, reversing the sequence by starting with just the bass string, moving to bass and middle together, then all three strings. Try the exercise with the first strum in, then again with the first strum out.

Below are flatpicking exercises designed to increase the flexibility of the right hand by developing precision in its ability to play any particular note without hitting others. I find it helpful to keep the fingers of the right hand (those not holding the pick) slightly closed but not tense while flatpicking. This seems to make it easier to keep the right hand relaxed and gives a more pleasing tone. Some players brace their right hand while flatpicking by letting the little finger make contact with the dulcimer. If you brace in this way, make sure that the finger rests very lightly on the instrument and remains as relaxed as possible.

## Exercise #14: Flatpicking Patterns

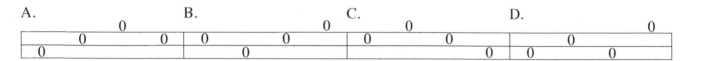

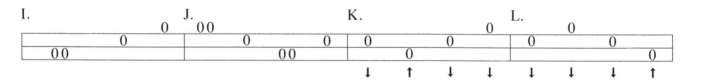

| Helpful Hints for Exercise #14 |
| --- |

- Change the direction of the pick (alternate inward picks and outward picks) for each note on all of these exercises.

- Repeat each section as often as you want, but at least five or six times.

- Vary the dynamic level as you repeat each exercise. That is, play it loud one time and soft the next. In addition to increasing your ability to play expressively, varying dynamic level builds strength.

- Exercises K and L are the same as B and C except several notes in a row are played with the pick moving in the same direction instead of alternating in and out.

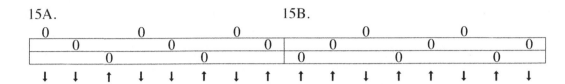

# Exercise #15: Crosspicking (A) and Reverse Crosspicking (B)

15A.                                              15B.

| 0 | | 0 | | 0 | | | | 0 | | 0 | |
| 0 | | 0 | | 0 | | 0 | | 0 | | 0 |
| | 0 | | 0 | | 0 | 0 | | 0 | | 0 | |

↓ ↓ ↑ ↓ ↓ ↑ ↓ ↑ ↑ ↑ ↓ ↑ ↑ ↓ ↑ ↓

*Helpful Hints
for
Exercise #15*

- Crosspicking is a technique used by mandolin players that adapts easily to the dulcimer. The pattern is made up of eight beats arranged in two groups of three and a group of two, and can be used for accompanying songs and tunes by adding in notes and chords with the left hand.

- Pay close attention to the notated picking direction. This particular combination of inward and outward picks is what gives crosspicking its unique sound.

# Exercise #16: More Flatpicking Patterns

A.

| | 0 | 0 | 0 | 0 | 0 | 0 | 0 |
| 0 | 1 | 2 | 3 | 2 | 1 | 0 | 0 |

B.

| 0 | 1 | 2 | 3 | 2 | 1 | 0 | 0 |
| | 0 | 0 | 0 | 0 | 0 | 0 | 0 |

C.

| | 0 0 0 | 0 0 0 | 0 0 0 | 0 0 0 | 0 0 0 | 0 0 0 | 0 0 0 |
| 0 | 1 | 2 | 3 | 2 | 1 | 0 | |

↑ ↓ ↑ ↓  ↑ ↓ ↑ ↓   ↑ Etc.

D.

| 0 | 1 | 2 | 3 | 4 | 3 | 2 | 1 | 0 |
| 0 | 0 | 0 | 0 | 0 | 0 | 0 | 0 | 0 |
| 0 | 0 | 0 | 0 | 0 | 0 | 0 | 0 | 0 |

↓ ↓ ↑ ↓ ↓ ↑ ↓ ↓ ↑ ↓ ↓ ↑ Etc.

E.

| | 0 | 0 | 0 | 0 | 0 | 0 | 0 | 0 | 0 |
| 0 | 0 | 0 | 0 | 0 | 0 | 0 | 0 | 0 |
| 0 | 1 | 2 | 3 | 4 | 3 | 2 | 1 | 0 |

↑ ↑ ↓ ↑ ↑ ↓ ↑ ↑ ↓ Etc.

20

<table>
<tr>
<td>

*Helpful Hints
for
Exercise #16*

</td>
<td>

- Further flatpicking explorations incorporating a few left hand notes. Remember the left hand fingering principles discussed in Section Two.

- Change direction with the pick for each note unless notated differently.

</td>
</tr>
</table>

- You can try out these flatpicking skills on Tune 12, Harvest Home, in Section Eight.

# FINGERPICKING

Fingerpicking is covered in more detail in Section Five. Here are basic fingerpicking patterns designed to strengthen the right hand and encourage flexibility and precision.

## Exercise #17: Three String Fingerpicking Patterns

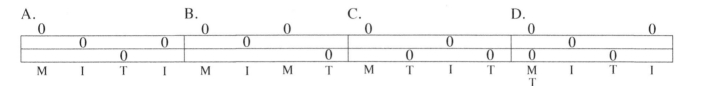

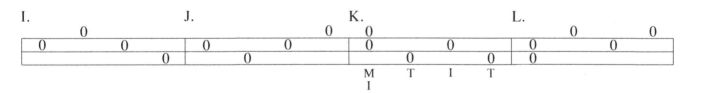

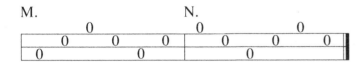

<table>
<tr>
<td>

*Helpful Hints
for
Exercise #17*

</td>
<td>

- In this exercise the middle finger plays the bass string, index plays the middle string, and the thumb plays the melody string. Some players do not use the thumb to fingerpick but play the melody string with index, middle string with middle finger, and bass string with ring finger. This exercise can be adapted to suit your fingerpicking technique.

</td>
</tr>
</table>

- Repeat each section as often as you want, but at least five or six times.

*This page has been
left blank to avoid
awkward page turns.*

# FOUR

## The Left Hand

The work of the left hand is almost entirely that of preparing notes for articulation by the right hand. Preparing notes involves stretching the fingers and placing them precisely into position, at the correct moment, to play the desired note or chord. The left hand has some involvement in articulation when slurring (hammer-ons and pull-offs) but has nothing to do with volume or tone. As obvious as it seems, it is sometimes difficult to remember that bearing down harder with the **left** hand does not help us play louder!

In Section Two, under the heading "The Basics of Left Hand Fingering" (page 9), are guidelines for left hand placement and fingering which are key to everything that follows in this section. Section Two also provides beginning exercises for learning and practicing these guidelines.

## SCALES

**For warming up and technical development.**

Scales are the basis of our musical language. One of the first tasks in learning any instrument is to discover where the various scales lie – both as a way of learning where the notes are and as a way of developing strength in the left and right hands while coordinating the two. A scale is simply a series of notes, arranged in ascending or descending order, that move from the starting note to a note that is an octave higher (or lower).

Scales are wonderful for warming-up as well as for further developing technique (practicing hand position shifts, for example), but they must be played consciously. Throughout this section I suggest different ways of playing scales that help keep them interesting. If you are bored playing scales, or lose the delight in playing them, either stop or play fewer of them. You work against yourself by playing scales without paying close attention.

**Pay attention!**

# Exercise #18: Lower Octave Scales

A. D Scale

| 0 | | 1r | | 2m | | 3i | | | | | | | | | | | | | | | 3 | | 2 | | 1 | | 0 |
|---|---|----|---|----|---|----|---|---|---|---|---|---|---|---|---|---|---|---|---|---|---|---|---|---|---|---|---|---|

| | | | | | | | 0 | | 1 | | 2 | | 3 | | 3 | | 2 | | 1 | | 0 | | | | | | |
|---|---|---|---|---|---|---|---|---|---|---|---|---|---|---|---|---|---|---|---|---|---|---|---|---|---|---|---|---|

B. G Scale

| 3r | | 4m | | 5i | | 6i | | | | | | | | | | | | | | | 6 | | 5 | | 4 | | 3 |
|----|---|----|---|----|---|----|---|---|---|---|---|---|---|---|---|---|---|---|---|---|---|---|---|---|---|---|---|---|

| | | | | | | | 3l | | 4r | | 5m | | 6i | | 6 | | 5 | | 4 | | 3 | | | | | | |
|---|---|---|---|---|---|---|----|---|----|---|----|---|----|---|---|---|---|---|---|---|---|---|---|---|---|---|---|---|

---

**Helpful Hints for Exercise #18**

- Here are two lower octave scales to start. Remember to keep back fingers down and work the fingers as a unit as described in Section Two. That is, in 18A when the index finger plays fret 3 of the bass string, the middle finger should still be in place on fret 2 of the bass. When descending to fret 3 of the bass string from the middle string (measure 4), place the ring, middle, and index fingers on the bass string at once (as a unit) on frets 1, 2, and 3.

- Change directions with the pick on each note, alternating inward and outward picks.

- Frets 1-3, the "lower octave," represent the most difficult position for left hand stretches. Refer to Exercise 5 for tips on handling this stretch. Thumb players may want to use middle, index and thumb to stretch over frets 1-3, but I also suggest working gradually to strengthen ring, middle and index in this position.

# Exercise #19: Scale Exercise in G

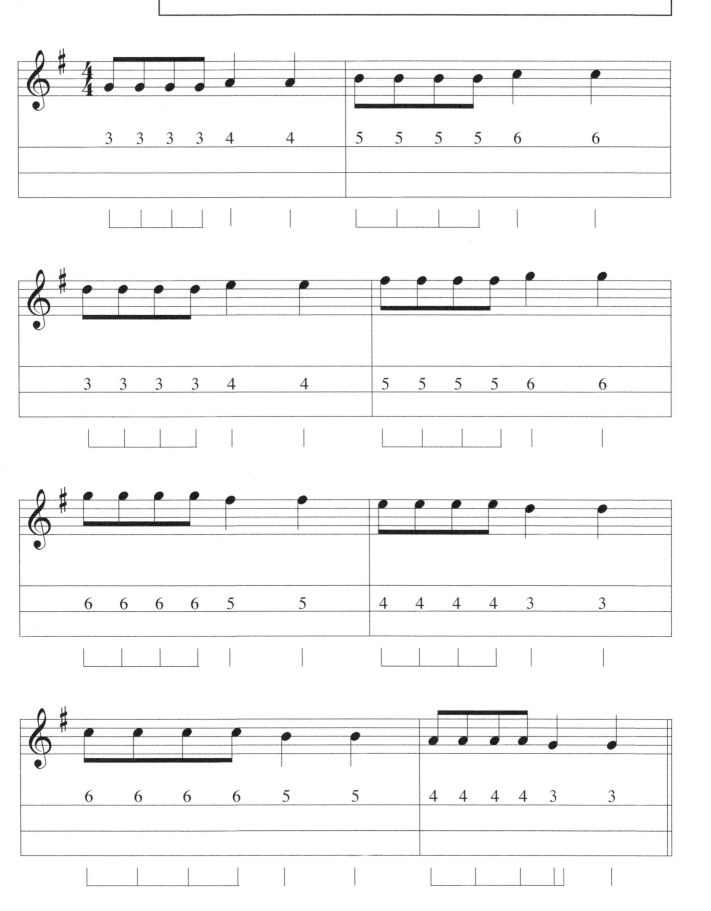

| *Helpful Hints*<br>*for*<br>*Exercise #19* |
| :---: |

- This is the companion to Exercise 5, in the key of G instead of D. You may want to review the tips to Exercise 5, which can be found on page 11.

- Use the same left hand fingerings as used for the lower octave scale in G, Exercise 18B.

## Exercise #20: Two Octave Scales in D-A-D Tuning

Here are six scales, each played over two octaves in D-A-D tuning. These are not the only ways to play these scales, as alternate positions for certain notes and different places to cross from one string to another could lead to a different pattern over the same two octaves. I include suggested fingerings, though these are also not the only ways to efficiently play these scales. I have notated these scales both in ascending and descending form. Play these very slowly and precisely to start. Keep back fingers in place until you have to move them. Exercises 20A, B, and D are written up one octave in standard music notation than actually played, by convention.

A. D Major Scale (Ascending)

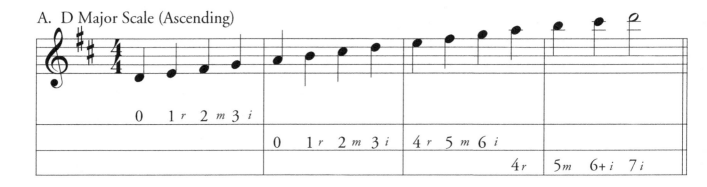

(Descending)

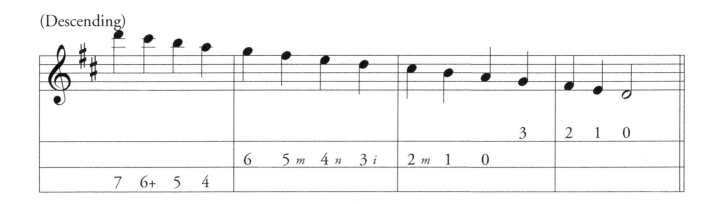

**B. G Major Scale**

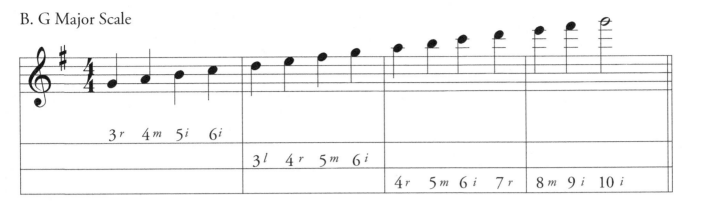

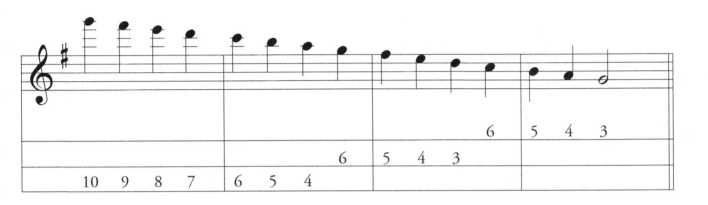

**C. A Major Scale**

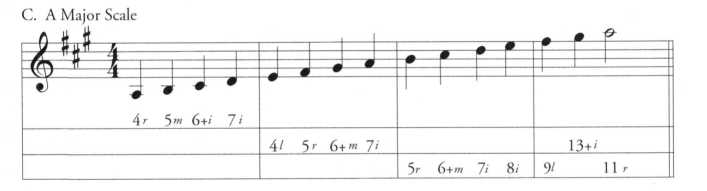

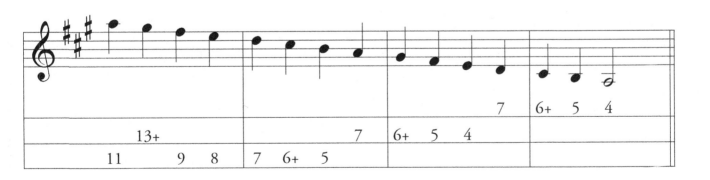

## D.  E Natural Minor Scale

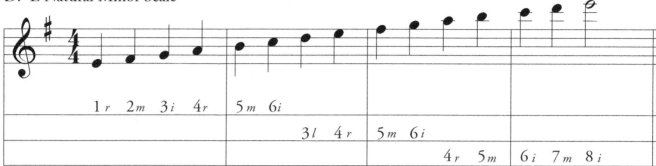

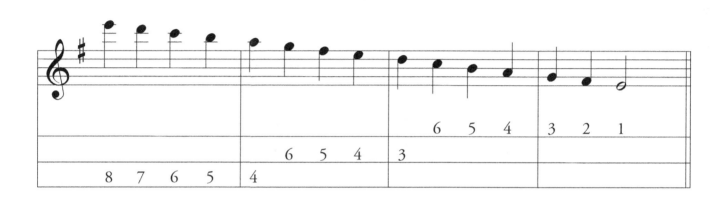

## E.  B Natural Minor Scale

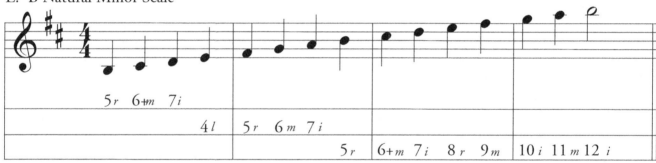

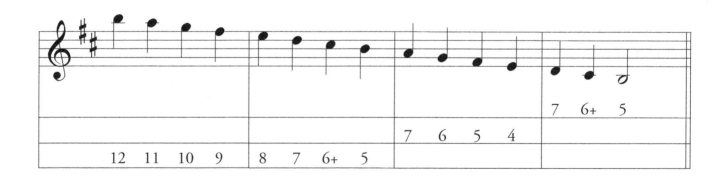

F. F# Natural Minor Scale

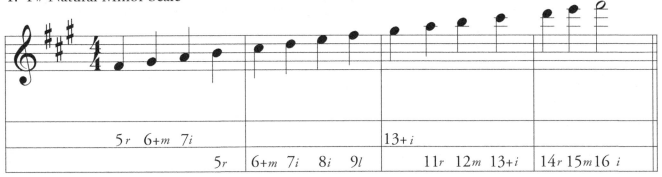

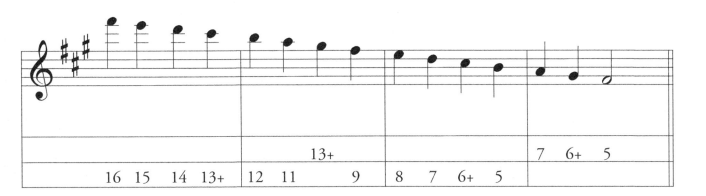

# Hand Position Shifts, Guide and Pivot Fingers

- Hand position shifts, where the left hand moves either from high on the fretboard to lower (or vice-versa) or from one string to another, are often the most difficult parts of playing scales. Its no surprise that position shifts are also one of the most challenging parts of playing actual music.

- Position shifts are made easier by using guide or pivot fingers. A guide finger stays on the same string, maintaining contact with that string, as the left hand shifts position. Having one finger remain on a string keeps your hand oriented on the instrument, aiding the other fingers in finding their positions. A pivot finger stays in the same place as the other fingers shift around it.

- In Exercise 20A, above, when moving from measure 2 to measure 3, the ring finger acts as a guide finger. After fret 3 is played by the index, both the index and middle fingers lift as the left hand starts to shift up. The ring finger maintains contact with the middle string while shifting from fret 1 to fret 4.

- A similar thing happens in measure 6 where the ring finger stays on the middle string after playing fret 4. The next note is index finger on fret 3 of the middle string. To get there, the ring finger moves from fret 4 to fret 1, and the middle and index fingers drop as a unit onto frets 2 & 3.

29

# Exercise #21: Guide and Pivot Fingers

A.

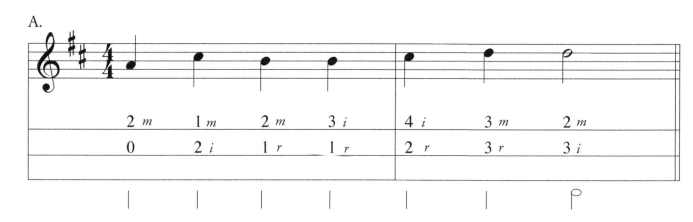

B.

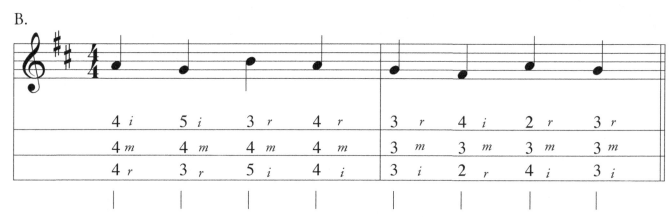

C.

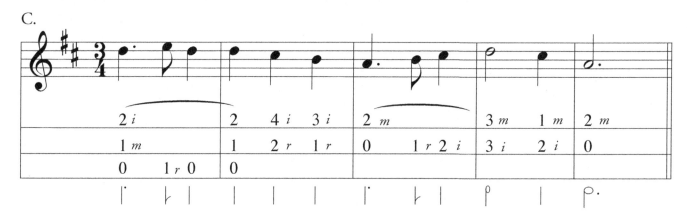

D.

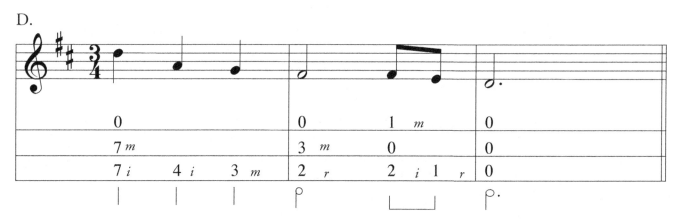

<table>
<tr>
<td>*Helpful Hints for Exercise #21*</td>
<td>

- In 21A, the middle finger of the left hand acts as a guide finger by remaining on the bass string through the first three chord changes. With the fourth and fifth changes the index becomes the guide until middle returns to the bass string for the last two changes.

- In 21B, the middle finger remains on the middle string where it acts as a pivot finger throughout the exercise. Follow the fingerings carefully and do not lift up the middle finger!

- In 21C the index finger functions as a guide for the first two measures, staying on the bass string. The middle finger then becomes the guide for the rest of the exercise, never leaving the bass string.

- In 21D, a passage from The First Noel (Tune 1), the index finger is the guide at first, moving from fret 7 to fret 4. The ring finger then takes over. To play the 1-0-2 chord on the third beat of the second measure, move the ring from fret 2 to fret 1 first. This stabilizes the hand and puts a back finger in position. Then, drop in the middle and index fingers to actually play the chord without lifting the ring finger. The ring finger is already in position to play fret 1, which follows the chord.

- To work on guide and pivot fingers in a piece of music try Tune 1, The First Noel, and Tune 3, Loch Lomond, in Section Eight.

</td>
</tr>
</table>

## Exercise #22: Scales at Capo 3

A. G Major Scale

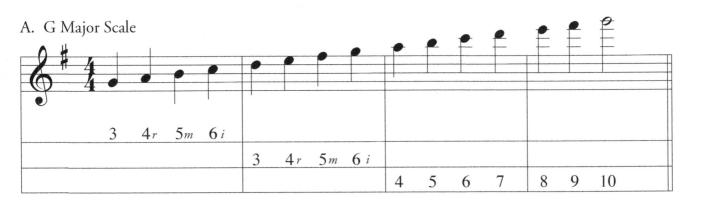

B. D Major Scale

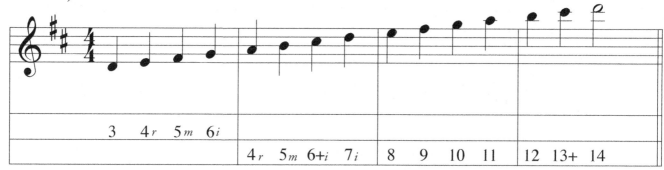

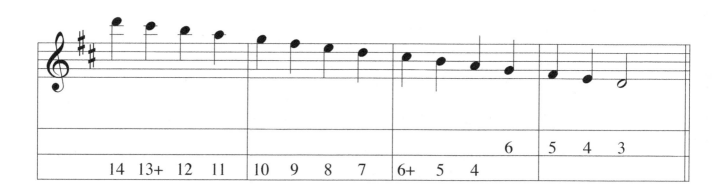

C.  E  Natural Minor Scale

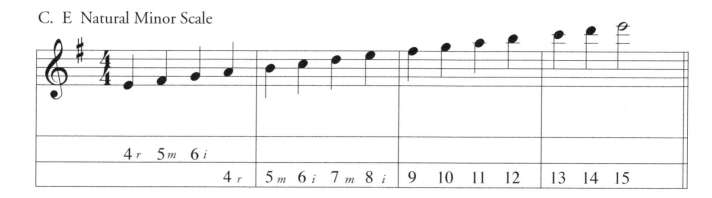

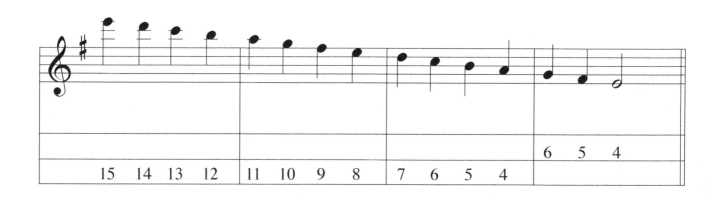

■ Three scales played with the capo on the third fret. These scales can be played without a capo as the actual notes stay the same whether there is a capo on or not. The capo limits the lower notes that can be played (nothing to the left of the capo can be played) and therefore the scales that are possible.

■ The pattern of the G scale in Exercise 22A might look familiar; the fingering pattern of the first two measures is identical to the beginning of the D scale in Exercise 20A. Fingerings in the key of D with no capo can often be transferred directly to the key of G with the capo on the third fret.

■ Remember that fret numbers notated with the capo are actual fret numbers, since the notes themselves do not change with the presence of the capo. Therefore, fret 3 equals the capo (which is placed at the third fret), fret 4 is actually the 4th fret on the instrument regardless of whether the capo is there, etc.

# Scales in Rhythm

■ Playing scales in different rhythms changes your perception of the notes as you set off each rhythmic group with accents. These scales present the notes in different groupings and are wonderful for working on smooth playing, expressiveness and hand position shifts. Tackle these scales only after you are familiar with the basic scales two octave in Exercise 20.

# Exercise #23: Lower Octave Scales in Rhythm

A. D Major Scale

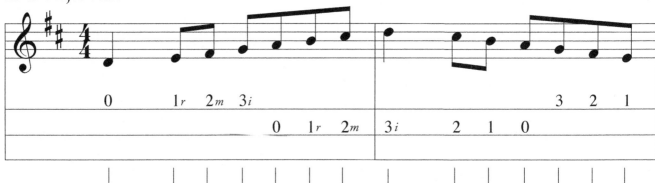

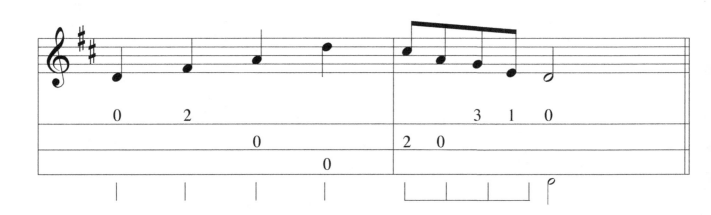

## B. G Major Scale

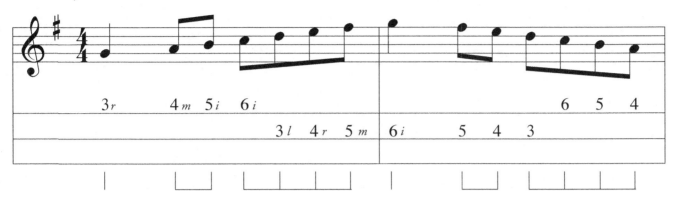

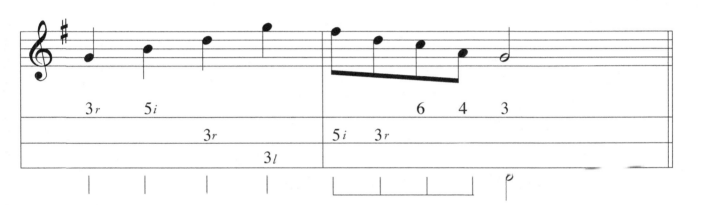

<table>
<tr><td>

*Helpful Hints
for
Exercise #23*

</td><td>

- Remember the basic left hand fingering principles (page 9) as you play this exercise. Keep back fingers in place (measure 1 of 23A, for example) and work the fingers as a unit (the end of measure 2 of 23A).

</td></tr>
</table>

# Exercise #24: Two Octave Scales in Rhythm

A. Scales in threes

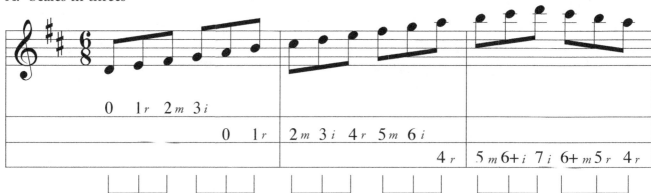

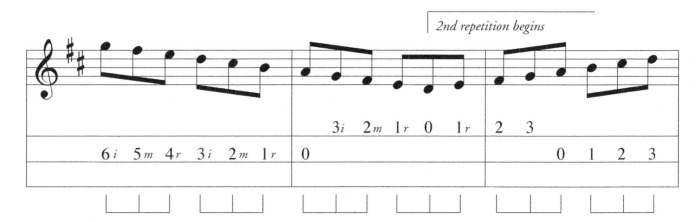

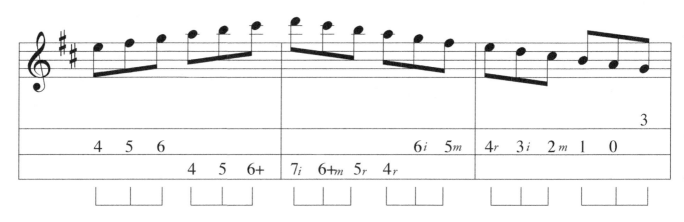

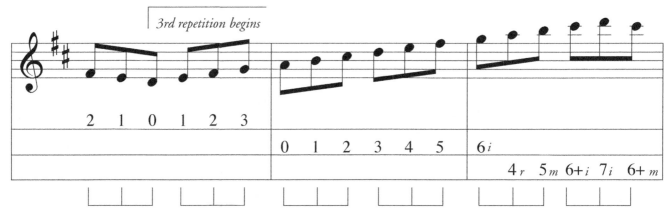

36

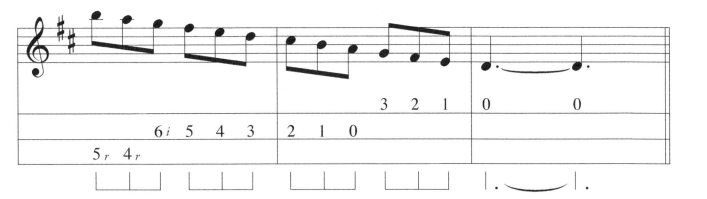

B. Quarters and Eights # 1

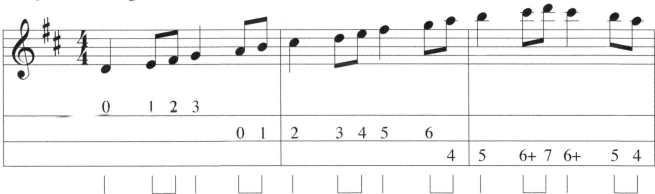

2nd Repetition starts:
continue with 2nd & 3rd repeats

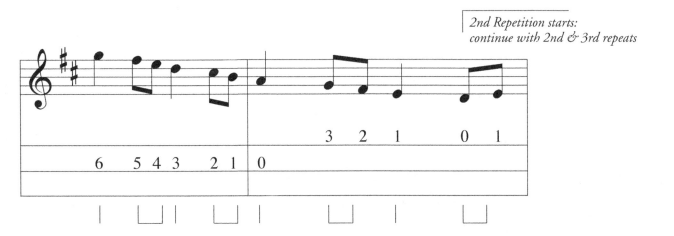

## C. Quarters and Eights # 2

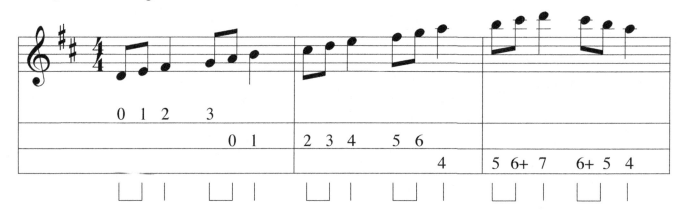

## D. Quarters and Eights # 3

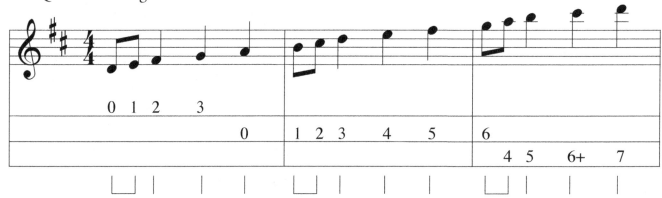

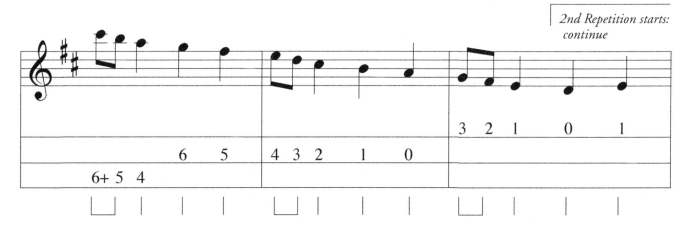

38

## E. Quarters and Eights # 4

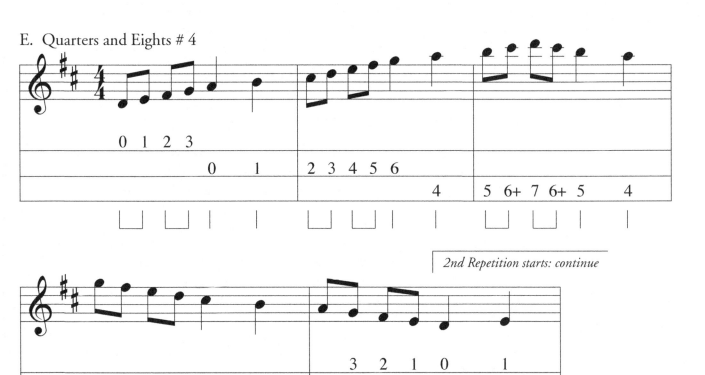

*2nd Repetition starts: continue*

## F. Eights and Sixteens

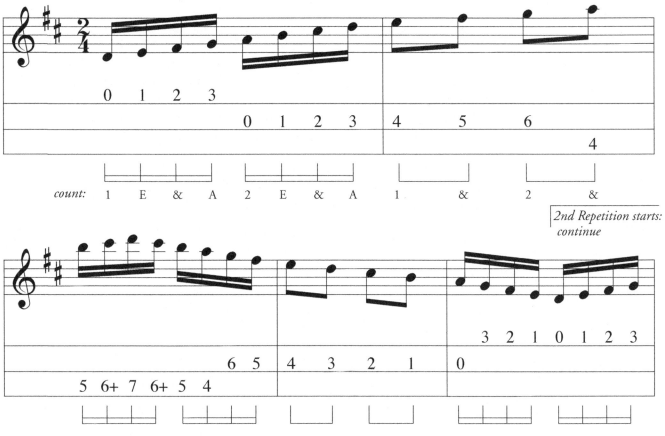

39

- The above exercises present two octave scales arranged in different rhythmic groups. Play each of these exercises three times (one time equals two octaves ascending and descending) to get the rhythmic groupings to come out evenly. Exercise 24A is complete, with all three repetitions notated.

- Accent the first note of each group of three in Exercise 24A. Try also accenting the last note of each group of three.

- After you are comfortable with these exercises, vary the dynamic level at which you play them. Play one repetition loud and the next soft. Play one measure loud and the next soft. Play a measure quietly, the next medium loud, the next loud, etc.

- On Exercise 24F (Eights and Sixteens) try playing the measure of sixteenth notes loud followed by the measure of eighth notes quiet. Then, reverse.

- These exercises are notated using the D major scale. Try them using any of the other scales you learned in Exercise 20.

- Change direction with the pick for each note. But, try Exercise 24A using the pattern "in, out, in" for each group of three. This gives two inward picks in a row when moving from one group of three to the next. For example the pattern for an entire measure would be: "in, out, in, in, out, in".

## Exercise #24A: Hand Position Shifts

- These are the tricky parts for the scales in rhythm. Here are a few suggestions for Exercise 24A:

- Measure 2, moving from fret 3 to 4 on the middle string: when playing fret 3 with the index, the middle and ring fingers are still in place on frets 1 and 2. Use the ring finger as a guide: maintain contact with the middle string and slide it up to fret 4. Practice this move without the right hand until the left hand can do it smoothly.

- Measure 4, beginning. When the index finger plays fret 6, middle and ring fingers should also drop as a unit into position at frets 5 and 4 so they are ready to be played.

# Exercise #25: Scale Fragments

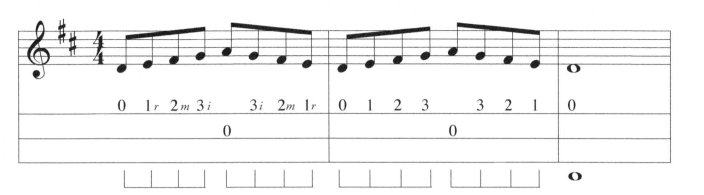

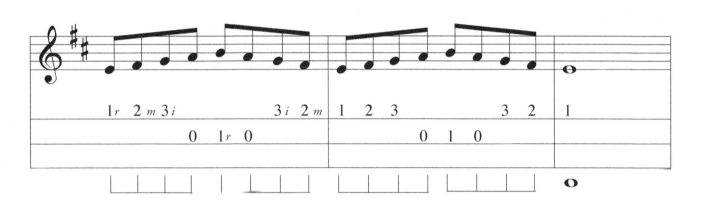

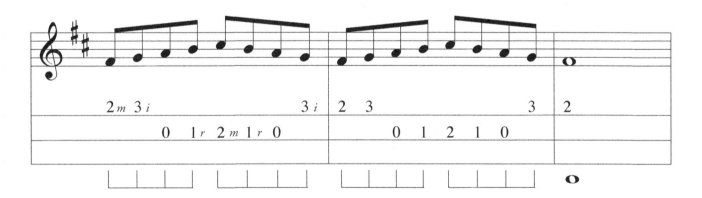

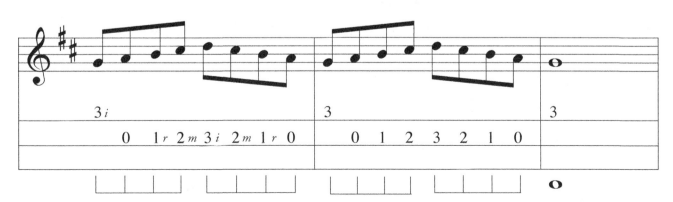

41

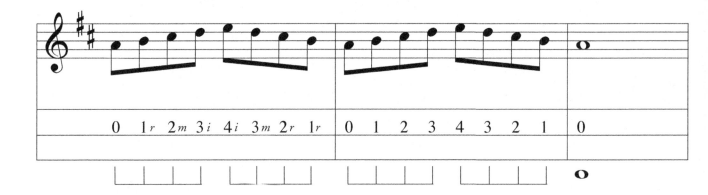

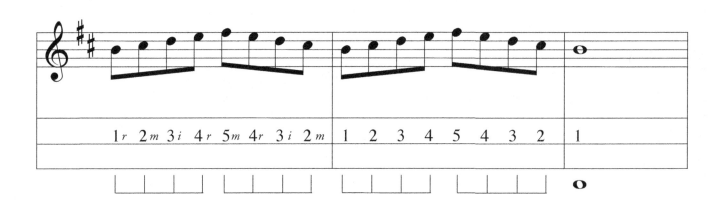

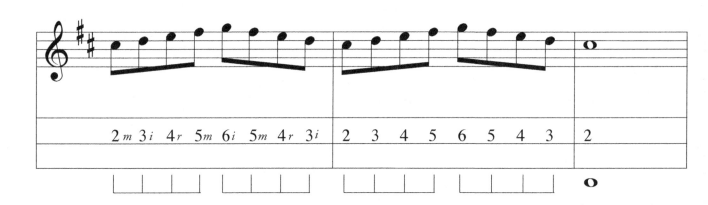

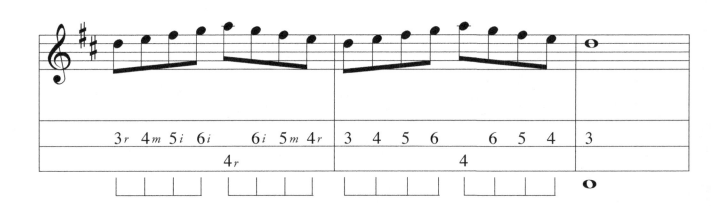

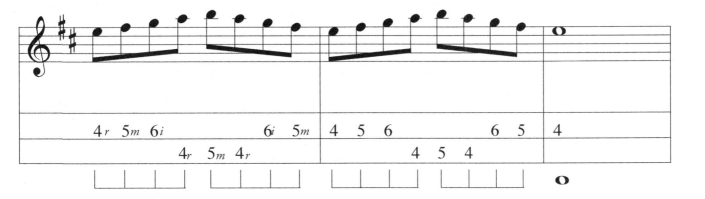

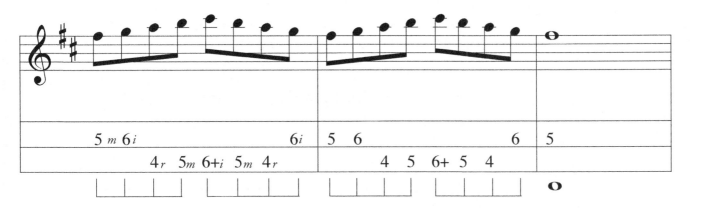

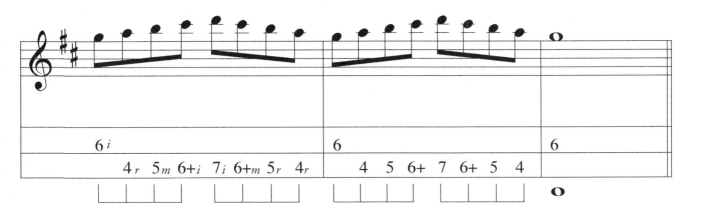

- Scale fragments are wonderful for practicing hand position shifts and for exercising the fingers of the left hand. To gain the most benefit from this exercise, play each section, and the transitions between sections, as evenly as possible. Let the whole note at the end of each section ring for a full four beats before moving forward to the next section.

- Remember to work the fingers as a unit and keep back fingers down whenever possible.

- Some sections may not seem efficiently fingered but remember that one of the purposes of this exercise is to practice position shifts.

# FINGER INDEPENDENCE

One key to effective left hand technique is developing the ability to maneuver the fingers independently of each other both up and down the fretboard and across the strings. The following exercises are designed to develop greater finger independence while improving dexterity and accuracy. They will also help the soft tissue in your hands stretch, increasing the distance you can reach on the fretboard. I urge you to proceed gently with these exercises. If you have small hands or your left hand is not yet well developed, be careful of putting too much strain on your hand. Start with just a few of these exercises and add more as you are able. If you feel pain, stop and rest. Finger fatigue is normal—pain is not.

The exercises are fingered for little, ring, middle and index fingers. I encourage you to develop the little and ring fingers, but players with small hands (or those who want to use their thumb) may also want to try middle, index, thumb on Exercise 26 and ring, middle, index and thumb on Exercise 27.

## Exercise #26: Simple Three Finger Independence

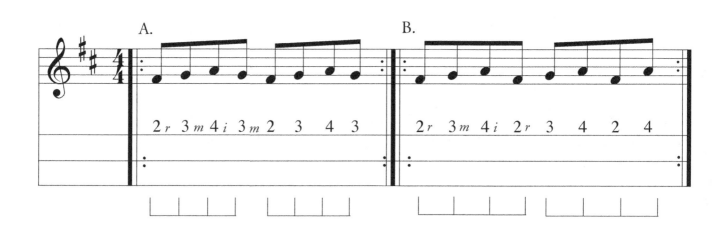

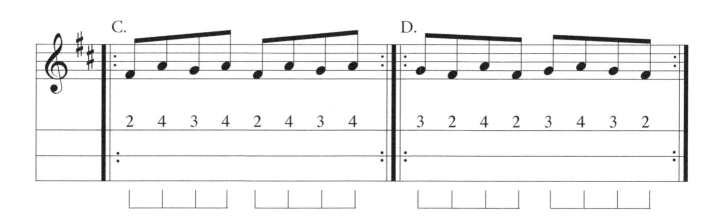

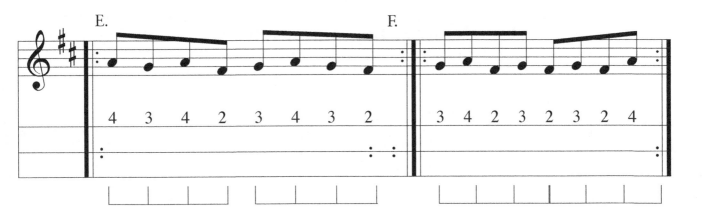

<table>
<tr><td>Helpful Hints<br>for<br>Exercise #26</td></tr>
</table>

- Fingering stays the same throughout the exercise: ring on fret 2, middle on fret 3 and index on fret 4. Keep the ring finger planted on the second fret for the entire exercise – it never lifts or moves.

- Keep back fingers down and in place.

# Exercise #27: Four Finger Indpendence on One String

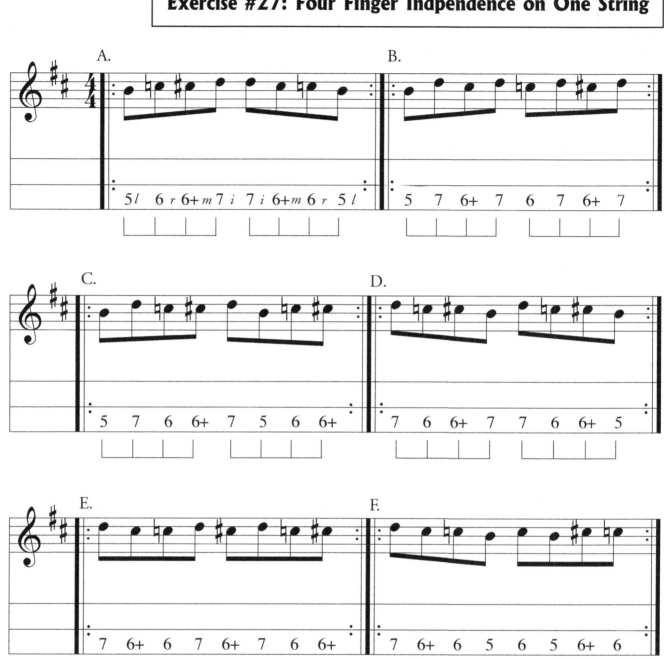

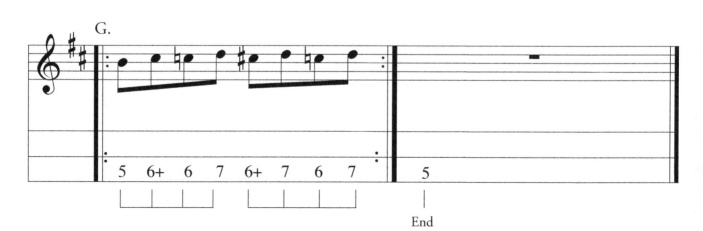

End

46

- Fingering stays the same throughout the exercise: little finger on fret 5, ring on 6, middle on 6+, index on 7.

- All fingers behind the finger making the note being played must be kept in position for this exercise to work. The little finger never leaves its place at the fifth fret – it should not lift up or move. When playing fret 7 with the index finger, middle and ring should also be in place at frets 6 and 6+, etc.

- Repeat each section before moving to the next section.

- Thumb players may want to also try using the ring finger on fret 5, middle on fret 6, index on fret 6+ and thumb on fret 7.

# Exercise #28: Finger Indpendence on Multiple Strings[x]

A. Four fingers moving

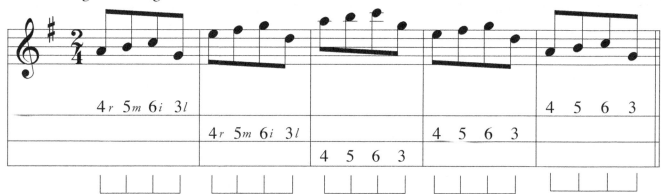

B.

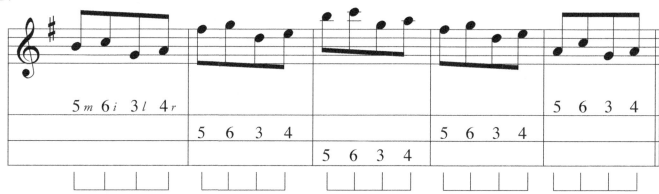

C.

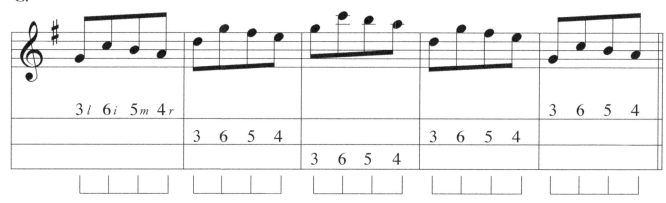

D.

E.

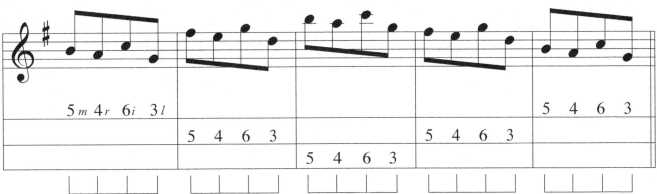

F. One finger stationary, three moving

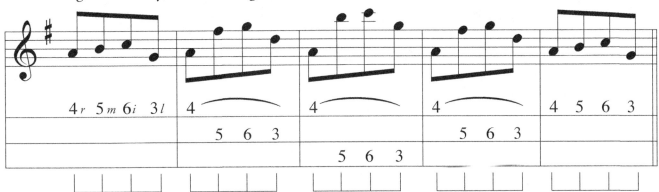

G.

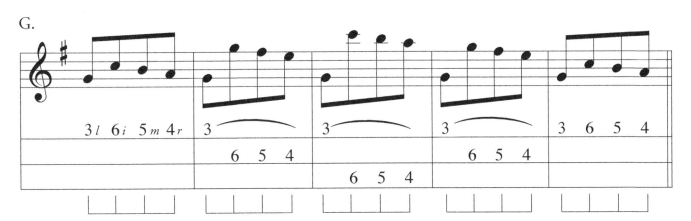

H.

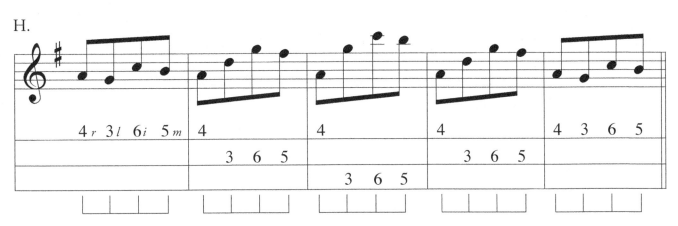

I. Two fingers stationary, two moving

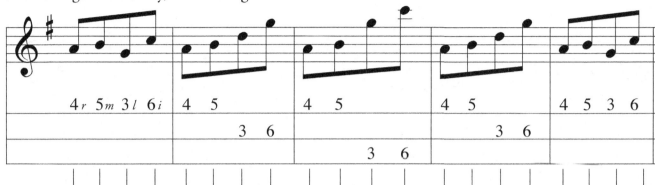

J.

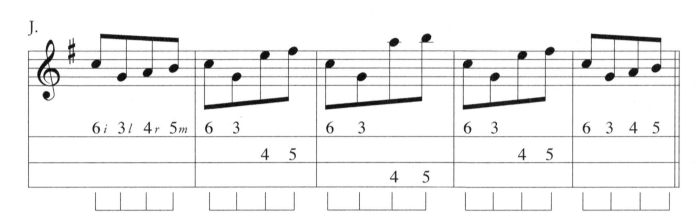

K. Three fingers stationary, one moving

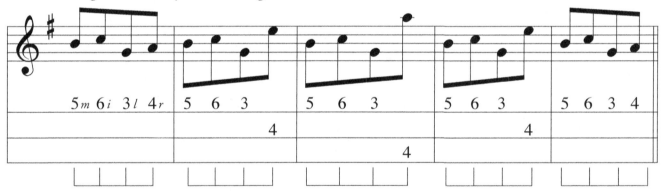

L.

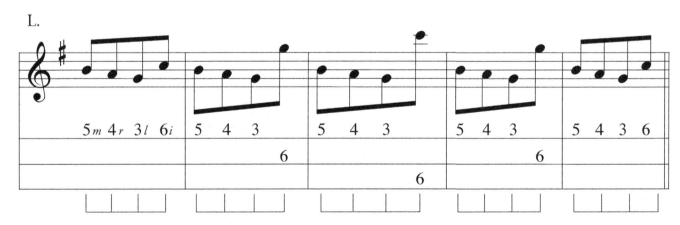

## M.  Changing direction, one finger stationary

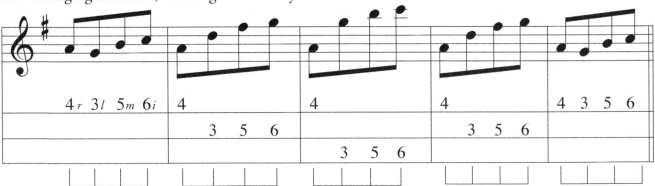

## N.

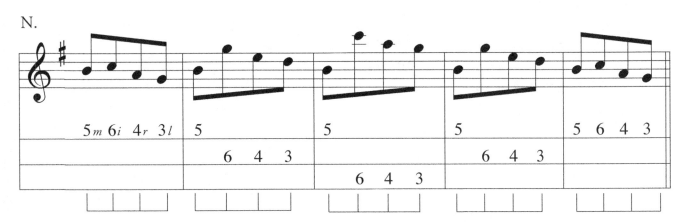

## O. Changing direction, two fingers stationary

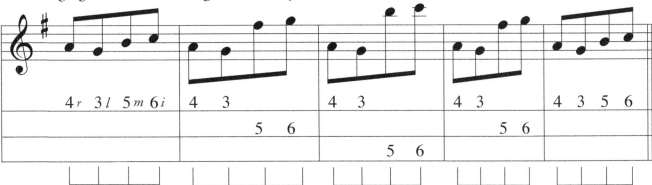

## P. Changing direction, three fingers stationary

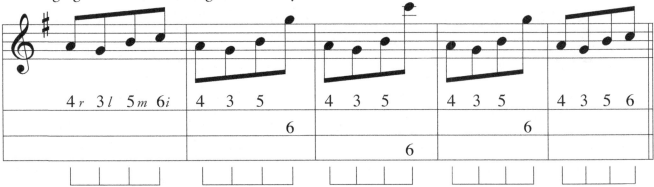

## Q. Moving between strings

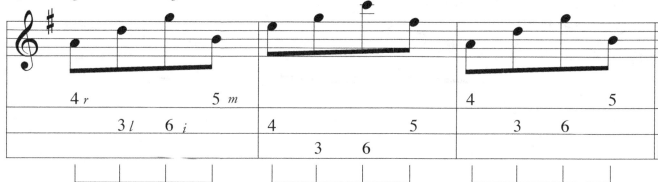

## R.

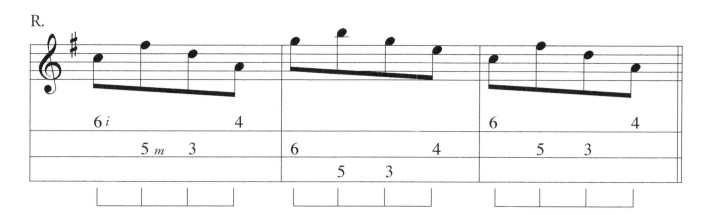

## S. Moving back and forth between strings

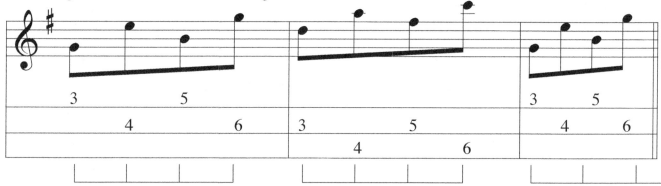

## T.

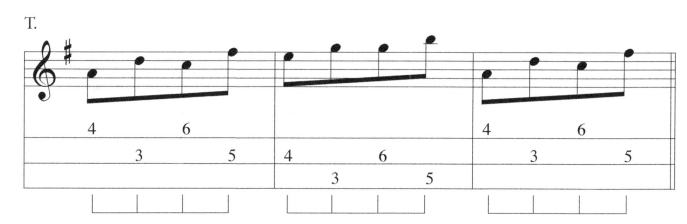

- Fingering stays the same throughout this exercise: little finger on fret 3, ring on fret 4, middle on fret 5, index on fret 6, regardless of which string is played.

- Starting in 28F, make sure to hold bass notes down as long as possible. Ties are notated in F and G to indicate these held notes – use the same idea for the rest of the exercise. In general, keep fingers in place until it is necessary to move them and hold as many fingers down at a time as you can.

# Exercise #29: Modal Independence

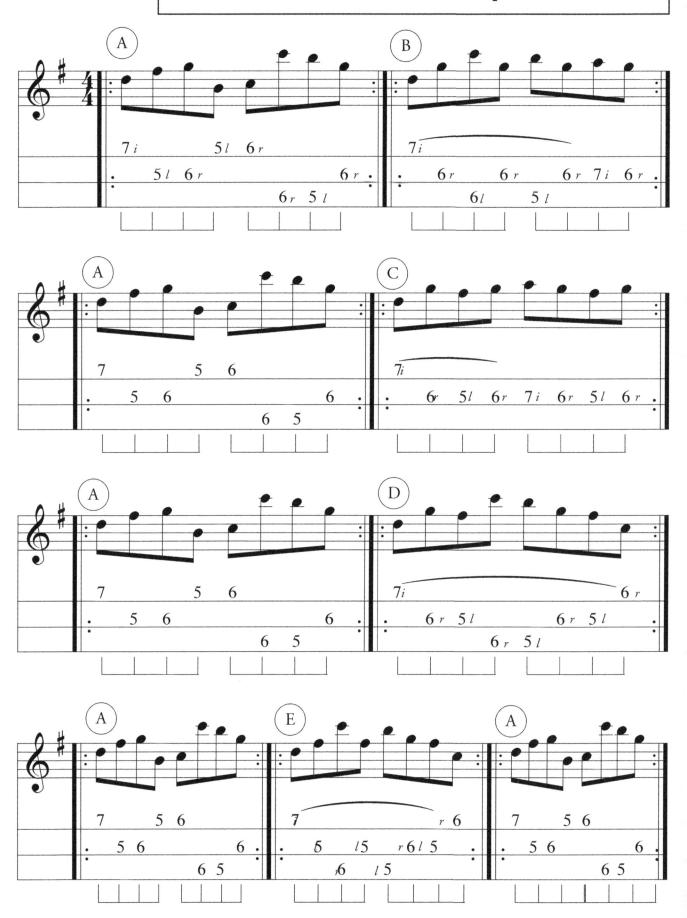

Helpful Hints
for
Exercise #29

- Two fingers, middle and index, remain in position on frets 6+ and 7 of the bass string for as much of this exercise as possible. (Even though fret 6+ is never played.) This helps strengthen and stretch the little and ring fingers which are doing most of the moving.

- In Section C, keep the little finger on fret 5 of the middle and middle on fret 6+ of the bass for the entire exercise. Do not lift or move them.

- In Sections D and E, middle and index can remain in position on frets 6+ and 7 of the bass string until the last note.

# Exercise #30: Modern Independence

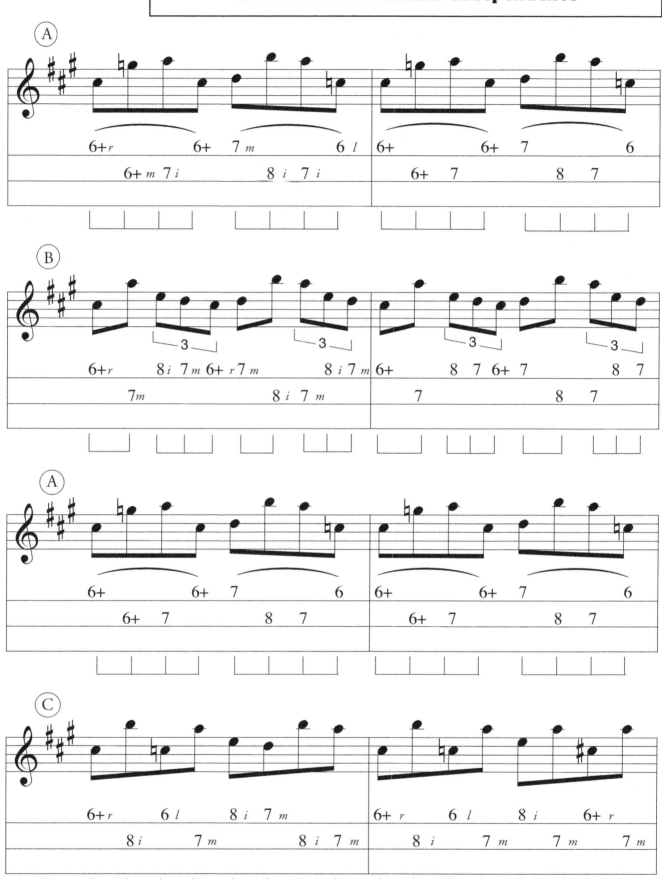

56

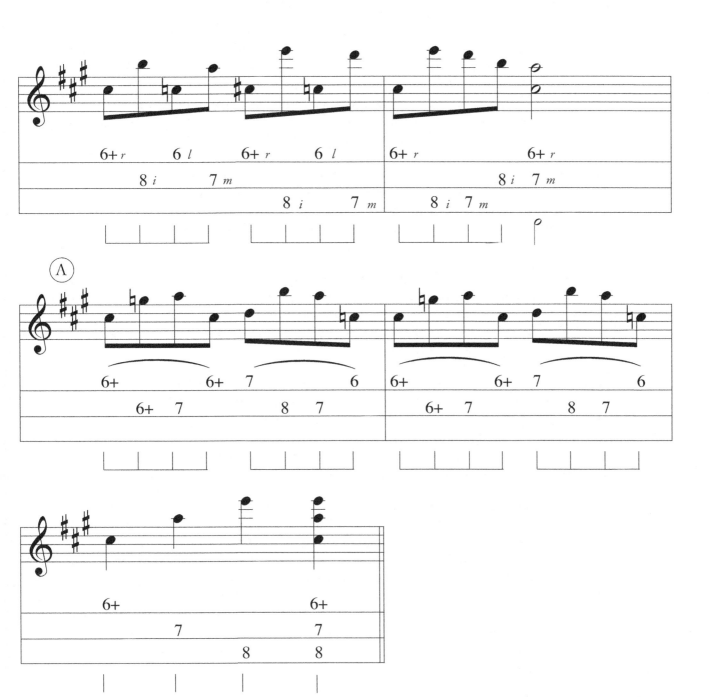

<table>
<tr><td>Helpful Hints<br>for<br>Exercise #30</td><td>▪ Two fingers, little and ring, remain in position for much of this exercise while middle and index move. The little finger does not move from fret 6 of the bass string and ring lifts only when little must be played. Otherwise the ring finger stays in place on fret 6+ of the bass.</td></tr>
</table>

# SLURS (HAMMER-ONS, PULL-OFFS AND SLIDES)

One simple way to define a slur is to call it two (or more) notes for the price of one. The first note is articulated (struck with pick or finger) with the right hand; second and further notes, different in pitch from the first, are not articulated but are produced by "snapping" down or off with the fingers of the left hand or by sliding from one fret to another. Ascending slurs (non-slides) for stringed instruments have acquired the name hammer-ons in folk tradition while descending slurs are commonly called pull-offs.

Notes marked as slurs are to be played together as a group with only one articulation. The most obvious effect is a smoother, more legato transition from note to note than even the most perfect right hand attack can provide. Slurs can also aid in playing faster music – taking out right hand articulation makes it technically easier to play fast.

**Playing Hammer-ons**

Playing ascending slurs, or hammer-ons, requires a sharp hammer-like striking of the string by the left hand finger tip. Accuracy matters more than strength, and it is crucial to land on the tip of the finger so that good hand position is maintained (page 9). The primary movement comes from the knuckle joint, and ideally the second note will sound as loud as the first.

Playing pull-offs requires a different technique: the lead finger is snapped off the string with the primary movement coming from the middle joint of the finger. It is important not to lift the finger straight up – this gives a very weak sounding second note – but to snap the finger towards the palm while the back finger (fretting the second note of the series) remains firmly in place. The finger pulling off moves into the fingerboard and towards the next string closer to you.

**Playing Pull-offs**

**Playing Slides**

Slides are a completely different slurring technique than hammer-ons and pull-offs. To play a slide, strum or pick a note and then slide the finger on that note up (or down) to another fret without lifting the finger from the fretboard. Like hammers and pulls you get two (or more) notes for the price of one right hand articulation but the sound is very different--reminiscent of the traditional style of playing the dulcimer with a noter. Two things to remember when sliding: first, make sure that you slide into a good fretting position with your finger just to the left of the fret you're aiming for. Second, look ahead in the music and see which finger you want to have in place at the fret you are sliding to (in order to be in position for what comes next) and slide with that finger.

## Exercise #31: Simple Hammers and Pulls

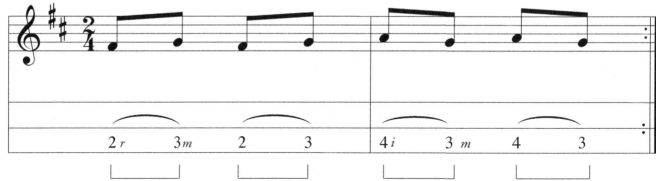

| Helpful Hints for Exercise #31 |
|---|

- The ring finger stays firmly planted on the second fret throughout this exercise.

- Only the first note of each group of two is plucked. The other note is produced by the left hand through either hammering or pulling.

- Remember that if the fret numbers on the tablature move from lower to higher you have, by definition, a hammer-on. Higher to lower equals a pull-off. Slides can go in either direction.

# Exercise #32: Hammers and Pulls in the Lower Octave

A. Lower Octave # 1

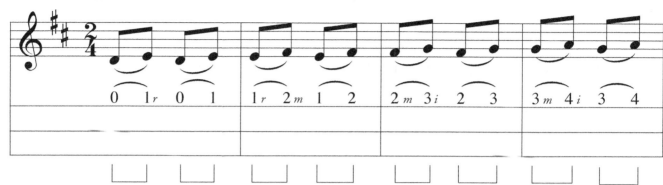

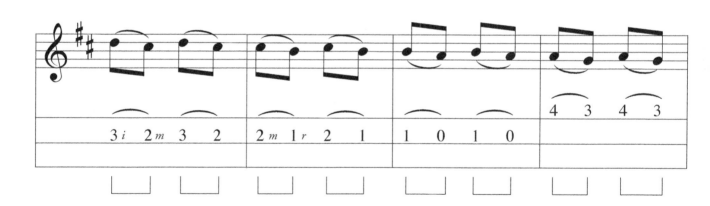

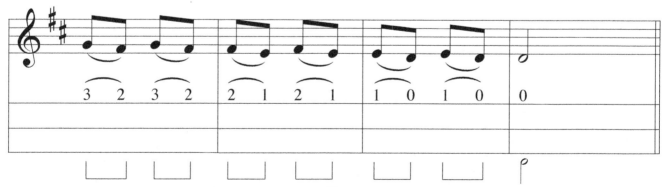

## B. Lower Octave # 2

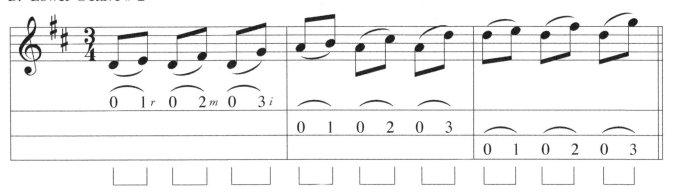

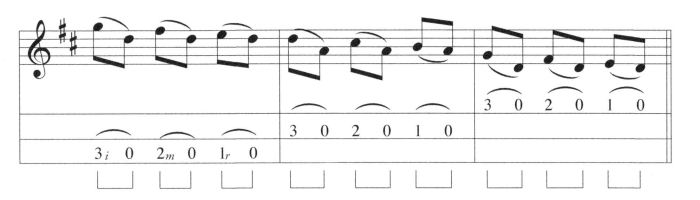

## C. Double Slurs

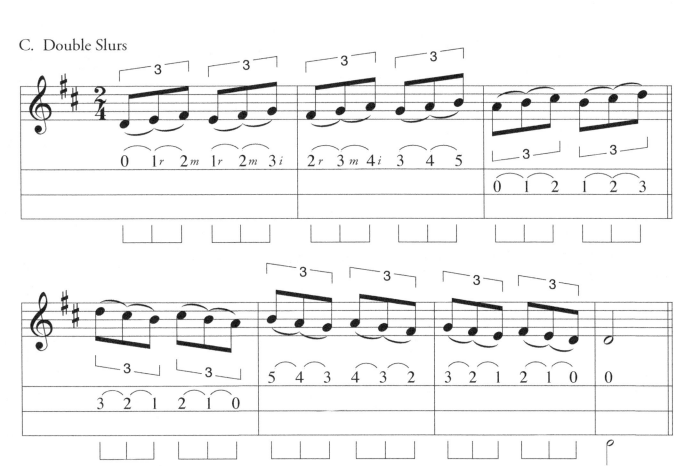

D. Hammer and Pull Combination

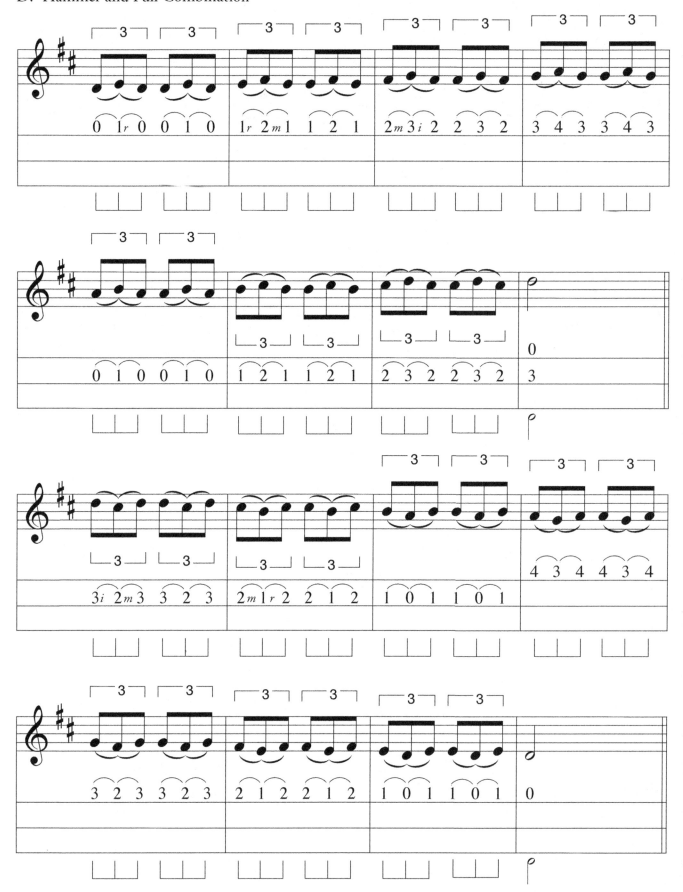

### E. Hammers and Pulls Over Two Octaves

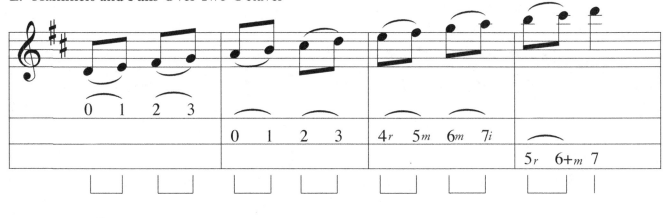

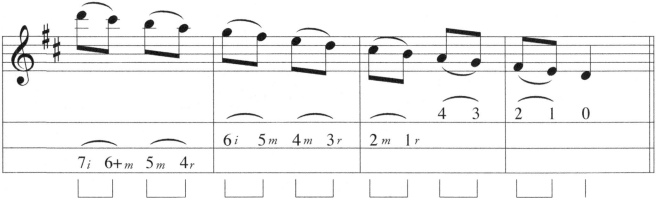

<table>
<tr><td>Helpful Hints<br>for<br>Exercise #32</td></tr>
</table>

- In the first half of Exercise 32C, each group of three is two hammer-ons in a row. Pluck once, then let the left hand produce the next two notes. The last half of this exercise consists of two pull-offs in a row.

- Index, middle and ring must all be in place before playing measure 4. The ring finger acts as a guide finger in measures 5 & 6. Slide it down from fret 3 to 2 to 1.

- The first half of Exercise 32D consists of groups of three with a hammer-on followed immediately by a pull-off. Pluck only the first note.

- To try hammer-pull combinations in a tune, play Tunes 7 and 12, Sally in the Garden and Harvest Home in Section Eight.

# Exercise #33: Hammers and Pull Exercise

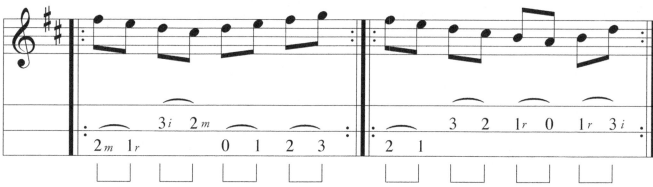

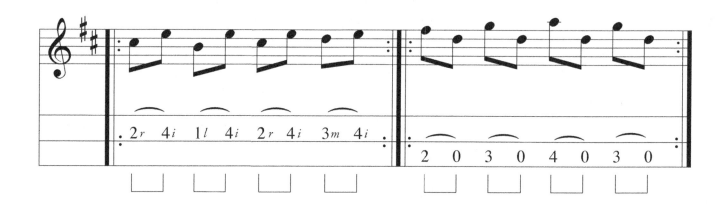

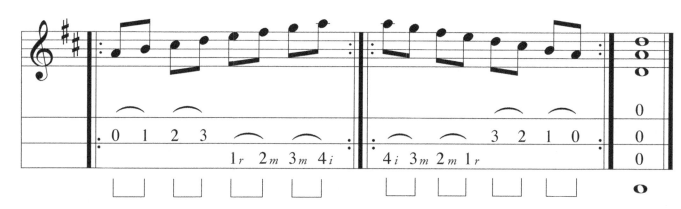

# Exercise #34: The Big Stretch Hammer and Pull Exercise[xii]

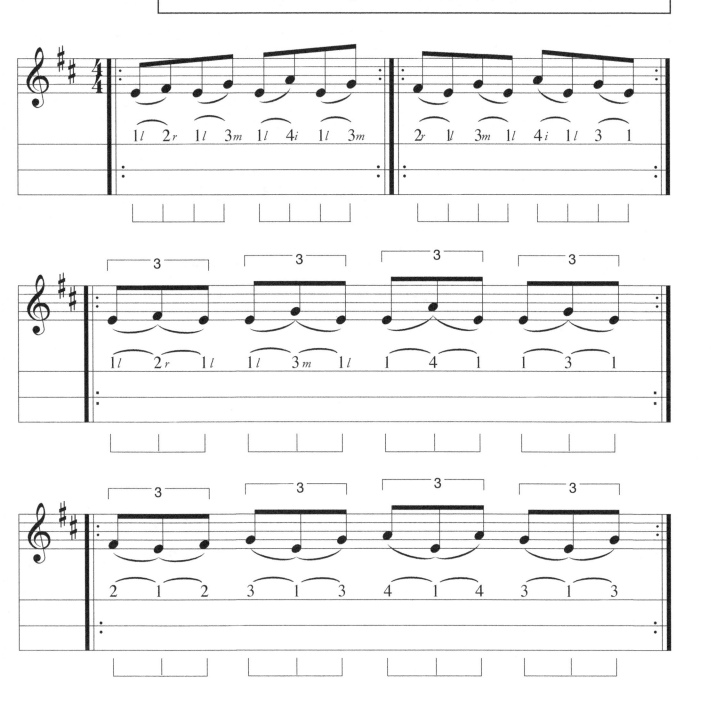

<table>
<tr><td>*Helpful Hints<br>for<br>Exercise #34*</td></tr>
</table>

- This is a wonderful though difficult exercise for stretching and strengthening the left hand. Plant the little finger on the first fret and leave it there – the other fingers will take care of the rest. This exercise can be done on any string and can also be executed further up the instrument to shorten the stretches. Simply plant your little finger wherever you want it to start.

- Also try this exercise by planting the ring finger on the first fret and using middle, index and thumb for frets 2, 3 and 4. This is not a substitute for the above fingering but a way to strengthen fingers used when playing with the thumb.

## Exercise #35: Slides

A. Slides up

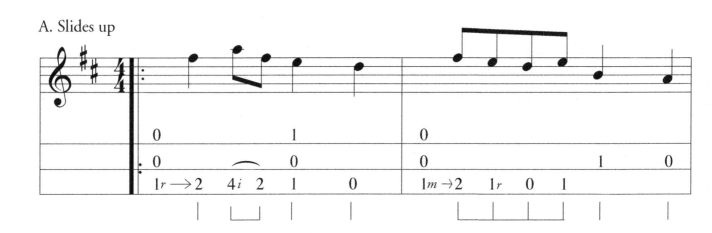

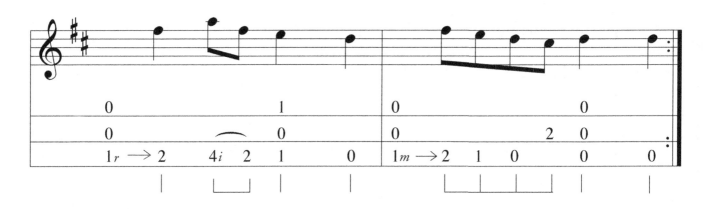

B. Slides up and down

67

- A slide is indicated with an arrow from the starting fret to the fret that is slid to.

- The first slide in 35A is done with the ring finger, leaving the index free to play fret 4 of the melody string. Even though the second slide is the same as the first, it is played by the middle finger so the ring finger is free to play fret 1 following the slide.

- The second slide in 35B moves down in pitch from fret 3 to fret 2. This slide also takes up a definite amount of rhythmic space equal to two eighth notes. The beginning of measure two has the same melodic figure, but the slur from fret 3 to 2 is handled by a pull-off rather than a slide.

- To experiment with different ways of articulating both with and without various forms of slurs, try Exercise 48, Articulation Choices. To practice slides in a tune try playing Tune 6, Shooting Creek.

# FIVE

## Fingerpicking

Using the fingers of the right hand to play individual notes, multiple notes and chords is known as fingerpicking. Using just the fleshy part of the finger (no nail) produces a soft, somewhat indistinct tone on the dulcimer. Many players prefer to grow out their nails or use finger picks to make contact with the strings. When using nails, the left side of nail (when looking at the back of your hand) produces a clearer, more pleasing tone than the middle of the nail.

## MECHANICS OF FINGERPICKING

**Plucking vs. Striking**

Classical guitar players, who have developed fingerpicking to a high art, differentiate between plucking and striking the strings. On the guitar, plucking involves the finger descending to the string, pausing, then ascending as it grabs hold of the string. This produces choppy playing and poor tone. On the dulcimer, reaching out with the finger and plucking up on the string is roughly the equivalent. Striking the string, on the other hand, produces a powerful, smooth sound with a pleasing tone. Striking implies that the finger begins its movement some distance from the string, accelerates, hits it a glancing blow and follows through. The primary movement comes from the knuckle joint which is the strongest and most flexible joint on the finger. On the dulcimer the movement of the striking finger, including the follow-through, is more towards us (parallel to the fretboard) than up and away from the instrument.

One good way to practice striking, and strengthen the knuckle joints of the fingers, is to play what classical guitarists call rest strokes. The rest stroke is so named because during the finger's follow through it comes to rest against the next string. On the dulcimer, using a rest stroke on the bass string brings the finger to rest against the middle string, while executing a rest stroke on the middle brings the finger to rest on the melody string. Rest strokes have a fuller sound because the finger sets the string vibrating more in the direction of the soundboard, resulting in added resonance from the instrument.

To execute a rest stroke, strike a string using the knuckle joint for power, then pull through the string until the finger comes into contact with the adjacent string. These strokes are, by definition, always towards you. Below is the same exercise we used for flatpicking in Section Two, also very useful for practicing rest strokes.

# Exercise #36: Practicing Rest Strokes

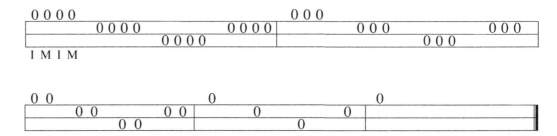

```
0 0 0 0                                   0 0 0
┌─────────────┬─────────────┬─────────────┬─────────────┬─────────────┐
│      0 0 0 0        0 0 0 0│      0 0 0            0 0 0│
│           0 0 0 0          │           0 0 0           │
I  M  I  M
```

```
0 0                    0                  0
┌─────────────┬─────────────┬─────────────┬─────────────┬─────────────┐║
│      0 0          0 0│      0            0          │              ║
│           0 0       │           0                 │              ║
```

*Helpful Hints for Exercise #36*

- Alternate fingers with each note to produce a smoother sound. Begin by alternating index and middle, then reverse next time through the exercise. Remember that each stroke is towards you.

- Strokes on the melody string are not really rest strokes since there is no adjacent string, but you can still follow-through with the finger.

- The thumb can also execute a rest stroke though it is in the opposite direction (away from you) from finger rest strokes. Substitute thumb rest strokes on the melody string in this exercise.

- To further practice rest strokes, use the scales in exercises 18 and 20.

*REMEMBER!* The purpose of practicing rest strokes is to strengthen the knuckle joint and encourage striking the strings rather than plucking, in order to obtain a more powerful and pleasing tone, and a smoother sound. Because the dulcimer (like the guitar) is difficult to play legato, anything we do to encourage smooth style and connected notes is a plus. During the course of fingerpicking actual music, most of the finger strokes will probably not be rest strokes, but free strokes. The movement for free strokes is basically the same as a rest stroke except the finger follows through towards the palm of the hand rather than coming to rest on the adjacent string. This follow-through is towards the back or heel of the palm so that the finger is not lifting straight up.

# RIGHT HAND POSITION

Fingerpicking on the dulcimer often involves "pinching" two notes with the thumb and either the index or middle fingers. In general, the thumb moves in a different direction than the other fingers – away from us rather than towards us. To achieve maximum strength for this opposing motion it is helpful to keep the thumb a little out of line with the fingers. If the thumb is lined up directly across from the index finger or to the right of it, the right hand is a little constricted and the resulting picking movements will be weak. Keeping the thumb a little to the left of the index finger takes better advantage of the hand's strong, natural movement from open fingers to a closed fist. Leaving the fingers free to move towards the palm of the hand without interference from the thumb enables much power to be brought to fingerpicking.

# FINGERPICKING PATTERNS

Exercise 17 in Section Three offered a number of fingerpicking patterns designed to increase the flexibility of the right hand. Below are a few more complicated patterns.

## Exercise #37: More Three String Fingerpicking Patterns

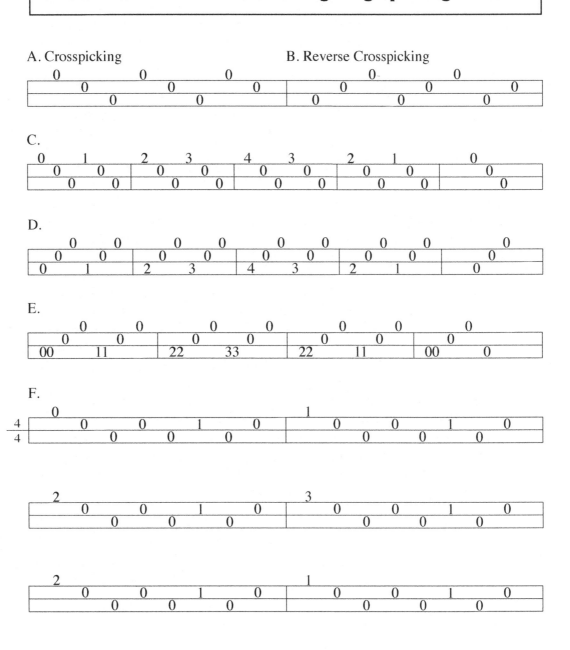

- Fingering for the right hand: Thumb plays the melody string, index plays the middle string, middle plays the bass string.

- Repeat each section of this exercise as often as you want, but at least two or three times.

## MULTIPLE NOTES

Playing two notes at once or chords (three or more notes) with the fingers is usually called pinching or brushing by dulcimer players, depending on the technique used. The term pinch refers to playing the notes together, all at once, using a different finger for each note of the chord. Often, pinching involves striking the notes with the thumb and either the index or middle fingers, or both if it is a three-note chord. Paying attention to the basic right hand position described above is especially helpful in achieving power and pleasing tone with your pinches.

A brush is a way of playing the notes of a chord in sequence, one after another, using just one finger or the thumb. Like strumming, the finger can play the notes of the chord nearly together by brushing quickly across the strings. Or, the finger can move more slowly through the notes of the chord so that it is arpeggiated. An arpeggio is a broken chord whose notes are played one after another, often starting with the lowest note and ending with the highest.

Brushes can be done with the thumb, either by brushing the thumb away from you across the strings (moving from the melody string to the bass string) or towards you (moving the opposite direction using the back of the thumb nail). Brushing towards you with the back of the nail can give a slightly harsher tone than other methods of brushing.

It is very effective on the dulcimer to brush towards you, moving from the bass to the melody string, using the index finger. This finger is easy to control, making it simpler to arpeggiate chords in whatever way is wanted. With the index finger it is also possible to use rest strokes for each note of the chord, producing a strong sound with full, rounded tone. Sometimes the middle finger can be substituted for the index brush if alternating fingers are needed.

Arpeggiating chords with a brush tends to produce more of an accent than playing the chord all at once with a pinch. Take this into consideration when choosing whether to brush or to pinch, perhaps using the arpeggiated brush when you want more emphasis.

# Exercise #38: Pinches and Brushes

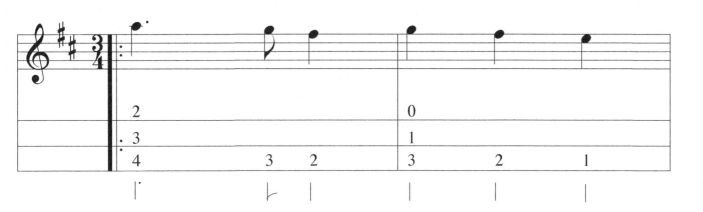

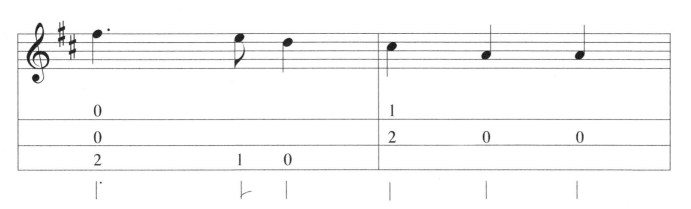

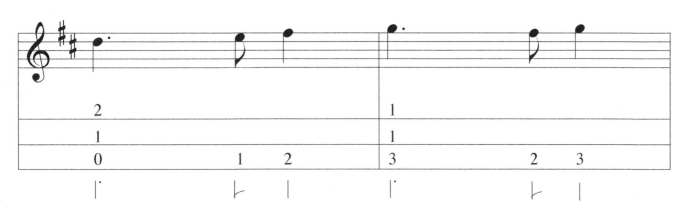

- Try this exercise first with just pinches and then again with just index brushes. Then combine the two and explore the difference in sound, effect and accent.

- Revisit this exercise after working through the next section on fingerpicking independence and play it without using the same finger twice in a row on the melody string.

To practice pinches and brushes in a piece of music try playing the fingerpicked version of The South Wind (Tune 8) and the Welsh harp piece Megan's Daughter (Tune 9).

# FINGER(PICKING) INDEPENDENCE

The left hand is not the only hand where developing the ability to maneuver each finger independently of the others is of prime importance; the right hand benefits greatly from this as well. The difficulty in assigning right hand fingers to always play certain strings when fingerpicking – thumb on melody string, index on middle, middle on bass, for example – is that eventually the music will call for playing the same string, or even the same note, twice in a row. Using one finger to play two notes in a row produces a choppy sound. There may be times when a choppier or more staccato style is desired but often dulcimer players want to play as smoothly as possible to overcome the non-legato nature of the instrument.

Classical guitar players alternate fingers when fingerpicking and dulcimer players can do the same. One difficulty for dulcimer players is that the melody is often played on the string closest to us, where the thumb is naturally positioned. But even here, thumb and index finger can be alternated to give a more legato feel, or index and middle can take notes on the melody string.

The following exercises are designed to encourage alternating fingers and develop right hand finger independence.

## Exercise #39: Alternating Index and Middle

| 000 | 000 | 000 | 000 | 000 | 000 | 000 | |
|---|---|---|---|---|---|---|---|
| 0 | 1 | 2 | 3 | 2 | 1 | 0 | 0 |

*Helpful Hints for Exercise #39*

- Use the thumb to play the melody string throughout; alternate index and middle on the middle string.

- Try Tune 10, The Munster Buttermilk, in Section Eight to work on alternating right hand fingers as demonstrated in this and the following exercises.

# Exercise #40: Easy Fingerpicking Independence Exercise

A.

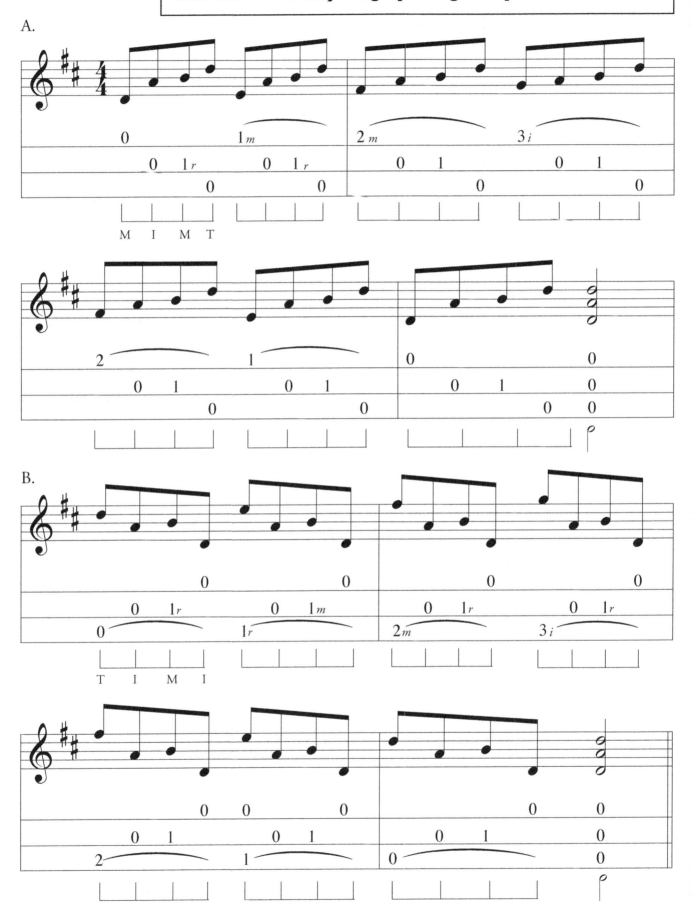

■ Remember that fingerings given below the tab staff in capital letters are **right** hand fingerings.

■ In 40A, right hand fingering stays the same for each group of four notes: middle, index, middle, thumb. In 40B the pattern is thumb, index, middle, index throughout.

# Exercise #41: Fingerpicking Independence Exercise

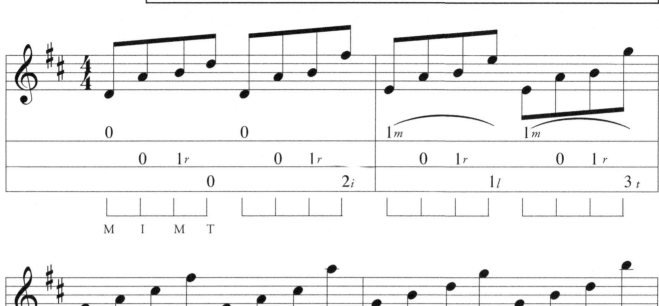

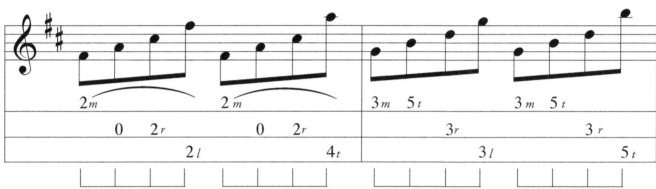

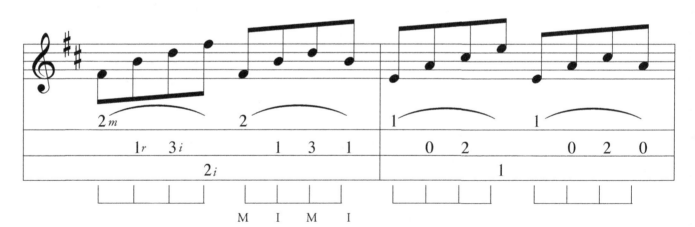

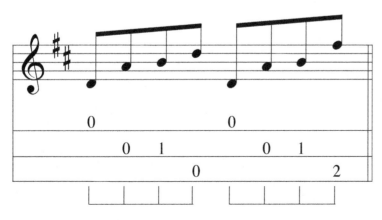

78

- Right hand fingering pattern is basically the same as in Exercise 40A: middle, index, middle, thumb for each group of four notes. In measures 5 and 6 the pattern changes slightly, as notated.

- Try Tune 8, The South Wind, and Tune 9, Megan's Daughter to work further on right hand finger independence.

# Exercise #42: Crossing Strings Independently

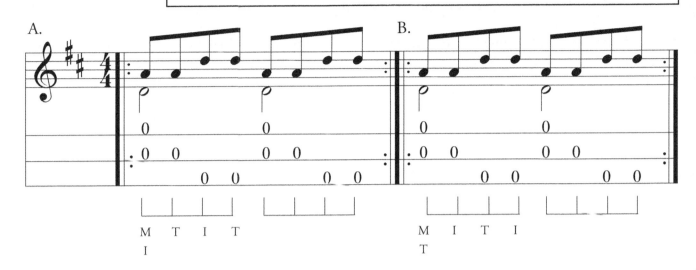

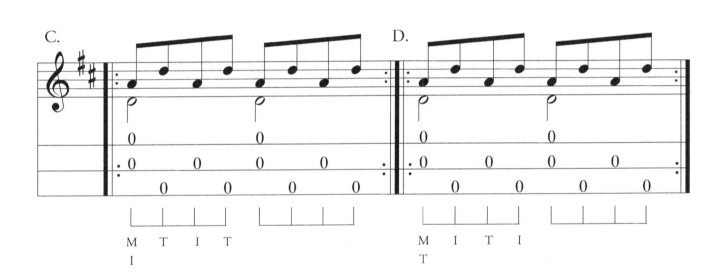

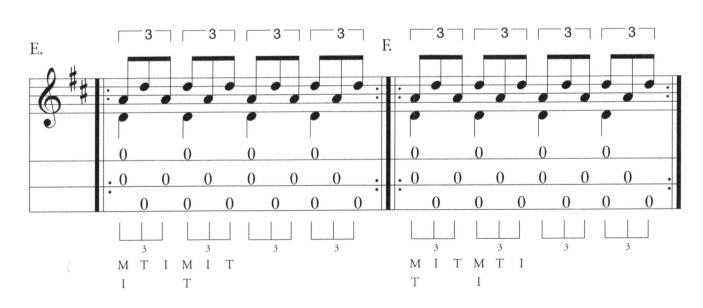

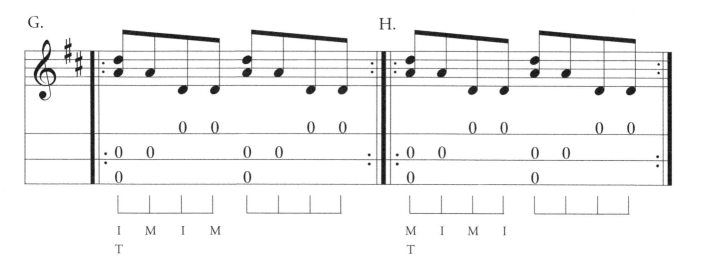

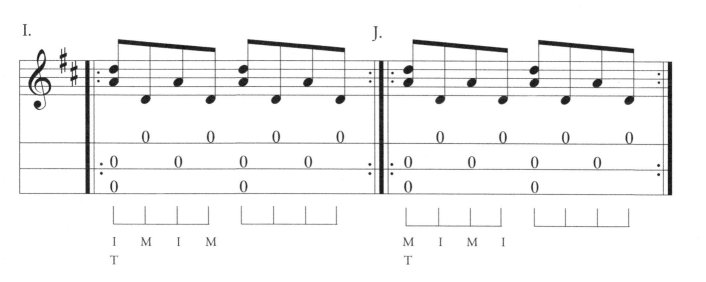

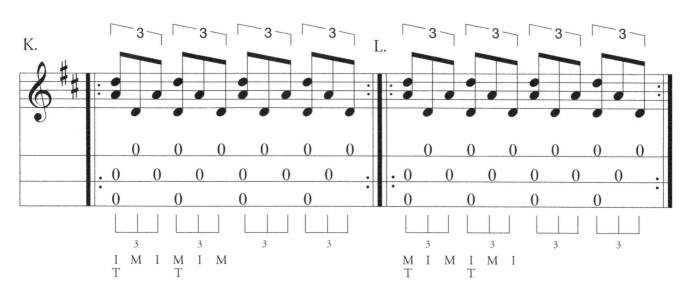

■ This exercise encourages right hand finger independence by alternating fingers and crossing strings. Pay careful attention to the right hand fingerings.

# Exercise #43: Fingerpicking Arpeggio Exercises

*(See page 88 for Helpful Hints.)*

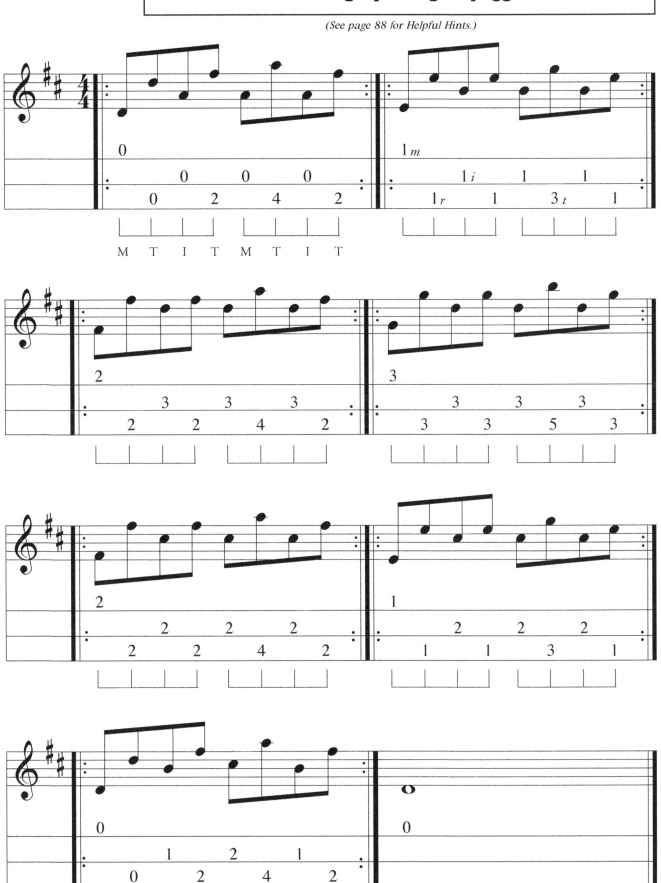

83

# Exercise #44: Traveling Arpeggios #1

*(See page 88 for Helpful Hints.)*

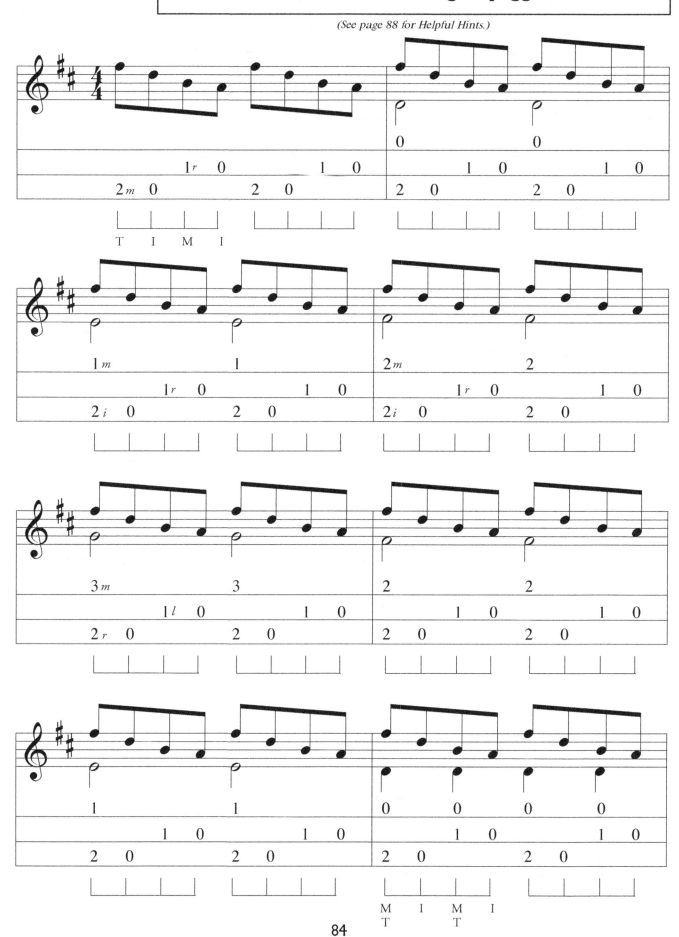

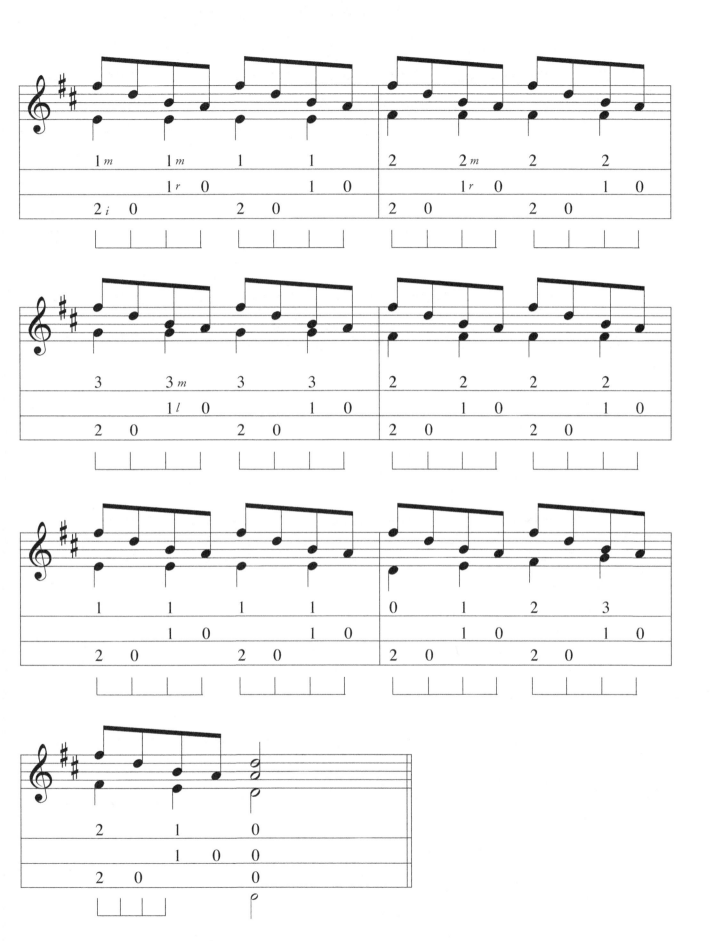

# Exercise #45: Traveling Arpeggios #2

*(See page 88 for Helpful Hints.)*

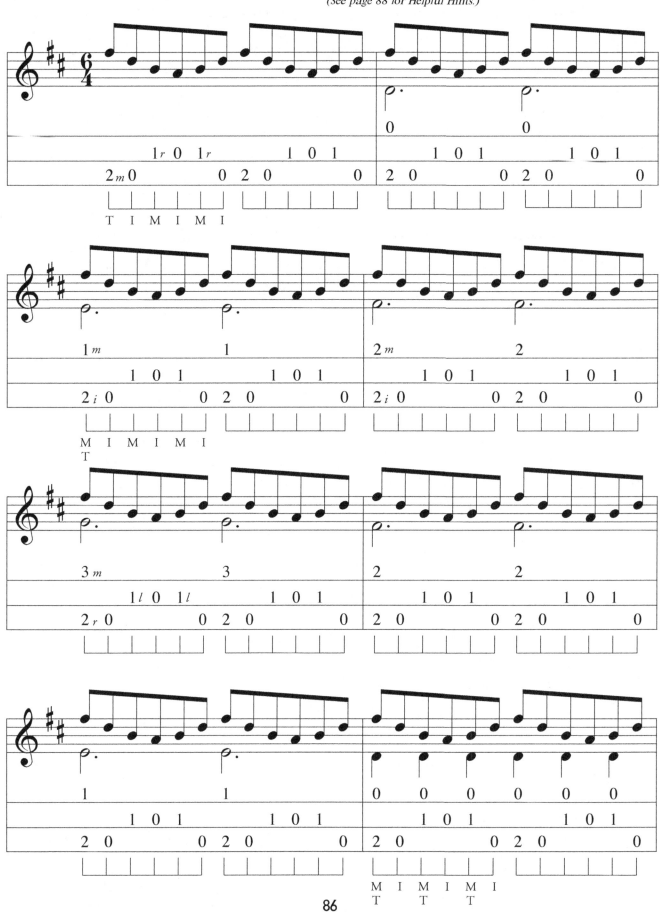

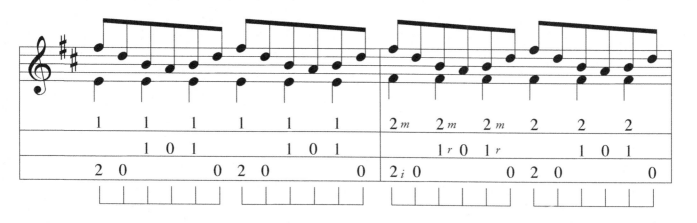

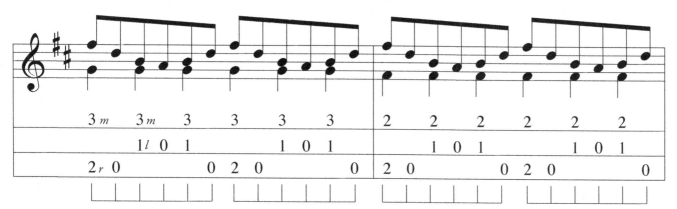

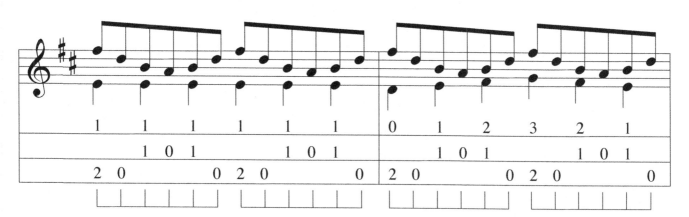

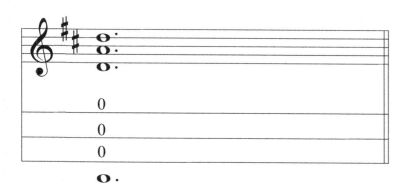

| | |
|---|---|
| *Helpful Hints for Exercise #43* | ▪ The same right hand fingering pattern is used throughout this exercise: middle, thumb, index, thumb for each group of four notes.<br><br>▪ At the beginning of the second grouping (centered around the first fret), the 1-1-1 chord is accomplished using the middle finger of the left hand on the bass string with ring on melody and index on middle. Place the entire chord at the beginning of the measure. Simply slide it up and down for the rest of the exercise. An alternate fingering for this chord formation is index on bass, then middle and ring. |

| | |
|---|---|
| *Helpful Hints for Exercise #44* | ▪ The descending melody in this exercise – F♯-D-B-A – stays the same throughout while the bass changes. Right hand fingers are alternated to achieve a legato feel. The picking pattern is thumb, index, middle, index and, later, thumb and middle together followed by index then thumb and middle together and index again.<br><br>▪ The middle finger acts as a guide finger for the left hand – it stays on the bass string throughout the exercise. |

| | |
|---|---|
| *Helpful Hints for Exercise #45* | ▪ This exercise is an extension of Exercise 44. Again, the bass line moves while the melody remains constant. The right hand fingering pattern at the beginning is thumb, index, middle, index, middle, index. In measure 8 the fingering changes to middle and thumb together followed by index, repeated three times for each group of six. |

# Challenges for both hands

This section offers more challenging exercises for either the right or left hand or both, and also addresses more subtle technical issues such as fingering choices, articulation, dynamics and tone.

## LEFT HAND FINGERING

All musicians have their own individual ideas on fingering, if not an entire fingering system. But even very different systems, if they are effective, share a common purpose (and probably a similar approach) -- to move from one point in the music to the next as easily and efficiently as possible so that the music itself speaks, rather than the player's technique.

Here are a few keys to an effective left hand fingering system:

**Keys to an effective fingering system**

• *Flexibility.* I advocate a five-fingered approach to dulcimer playing. If the left hand is developed enough to make possible the use of any finger from thumb to little to solve a musical problem, then there is a greater chance of successfully playing challenging music.

**Flexibility**

• *Consistency.* Any effective fingering system must address similar problems in similar ways. If you leave it to chance (whatever finger happens to be there will play the note), likely as not, either the note will not be played well or the fingers will stumble with the next note because they are in poor position. If you play a specific passage one way, play it the same way when you encounter it again. Use the same approach for similar passages.

**Consistency**

• *Preparation.* Left hand fingering is not just a matter of making decisions based on where you are in the music, but also looking ahead in order to place the fingers in such a way as to prepare for what is coming next. Use guide and pivot fingers as much as possible.

**Preparation**

• *Industriousness.* Don't be lazy. Consistently skipping a finger because it is weaker than another means you will never be able to use it. Glossing over a difficult section without breaking it down to solve its problems means you will never be able to play it.

**Industriousness**

Remember, no single fingering system is perfect, and the only goal is to produce music that is satisfying to you and your listeners.

Each section of Exercise 46, below, presents the same melodic material twice with different fingerings. When solving fingering dilemmas it can also be helpful to remember that the note you need may be found in more than one place. Crossing to adjacent strings can sometimes resolve difficult passages. Starting with 46C, the melody is notated on one string in the first measure while the second measure makes use of an adjacent string.

## Exercise #46: Left Hand Fingering Options

A.

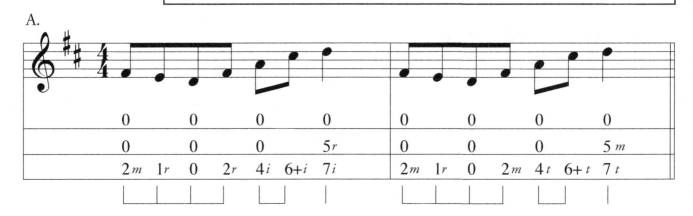

B.

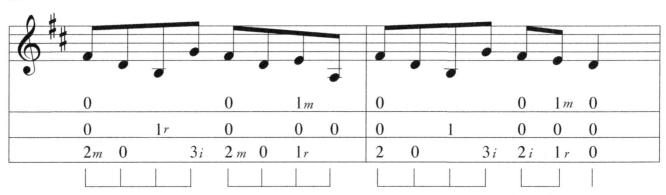

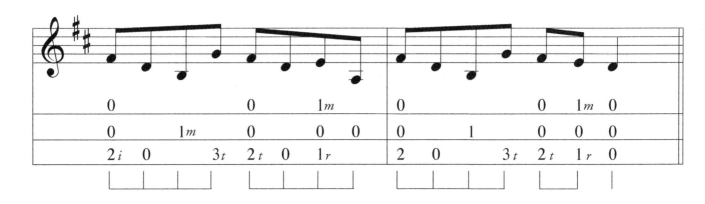

90

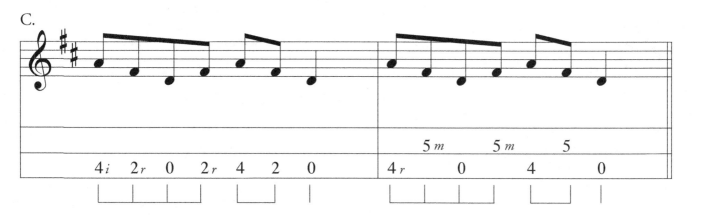

C.

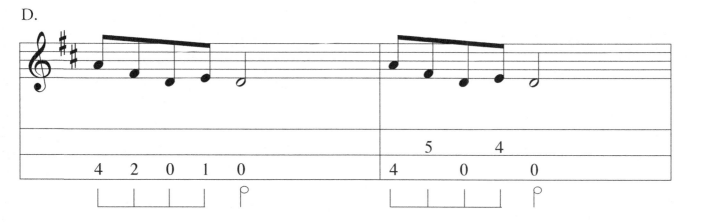

D.

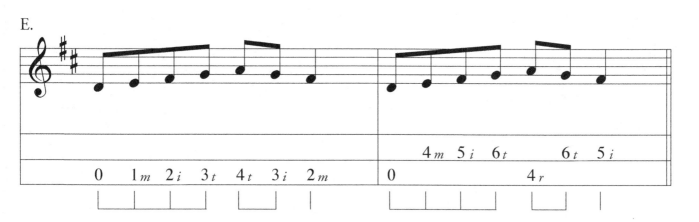

E.

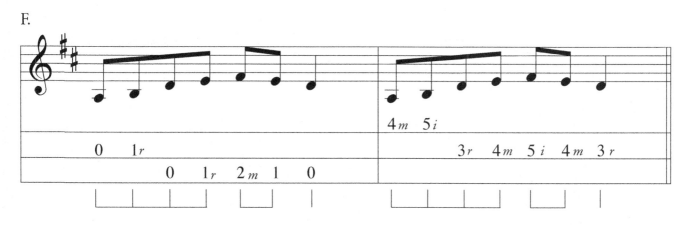

F.

91

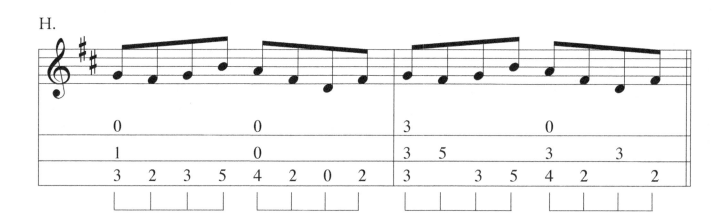

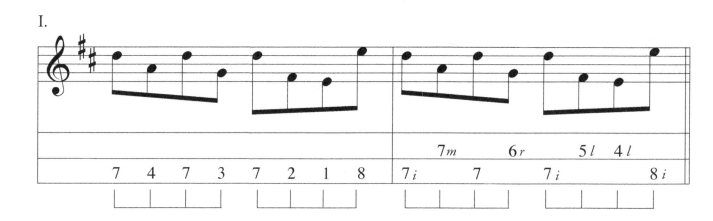

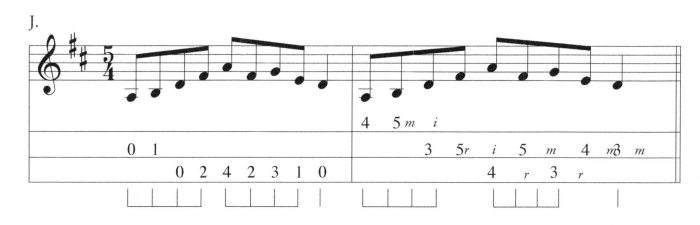

# Exercise #47: Intervals

A. Thirds

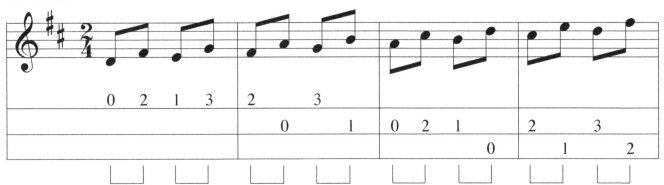

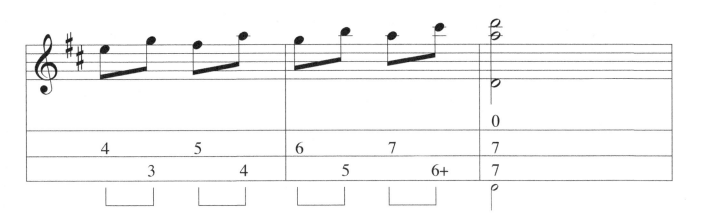

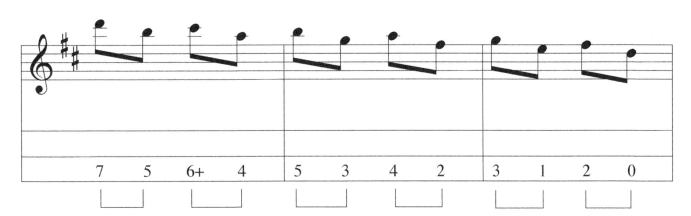

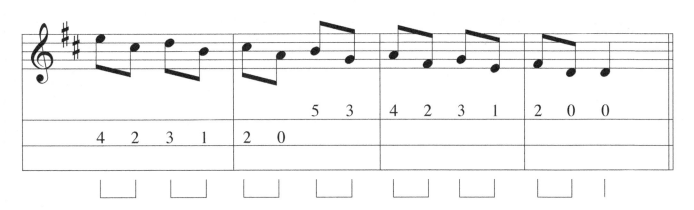

## B. Fourths

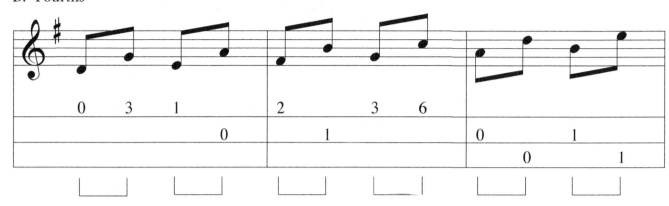

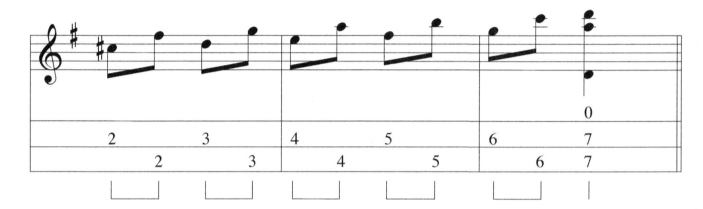

## C. Sixths

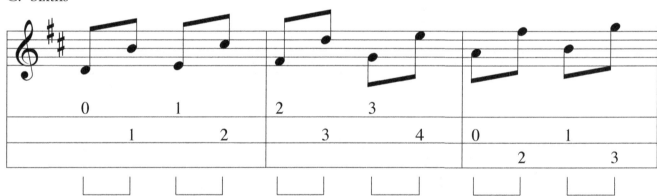

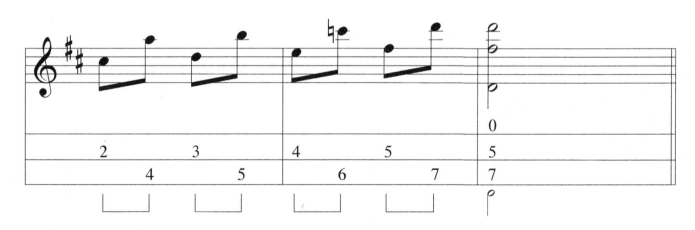

<table>
<tr><td>Helpful Hints<br>for<br>Exercise #47</td><td>■ Exercises A and C present both major and minor thirds and sixths.<br><br>■ Exercise A offers different fingering options ascending and descending.</td></tr>
</table>

# ARTICULATION (To Slur or Not to Slur)

One meaning of the word articulation is the manner in which a note is produced. On the dulcimer we produce notes by picking with our fingers or a pick while placing the left hand fingers on the frets desired. The pattern of articulation can be changed by slurring, where one pick with the right hand produces multiple notes from left hand hammer-ons, pull-offs or slides. Passages played with slurs have a more legato feel due to fewer right hand strikes, but also contain more finger noise from the hammering and pulling. Using too many slurs can result in passages that sound jerky and phrasing that sounds odd. In Exercise 48A-C below, the first measure presents a passage with no slurs; the following measures give examples of various ways to add slurs. No measure is right or wrong. Rather, it is a matter of individual taste which variation is preferred. Each measure sounds and feels subtly different. In 48D each measure has the same melody again but is articulated with a different combination of hammer-ons, pull-offs and slides.

## Exercise #48: Articulation Choices

A.

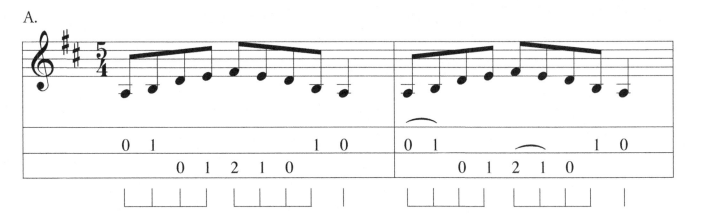

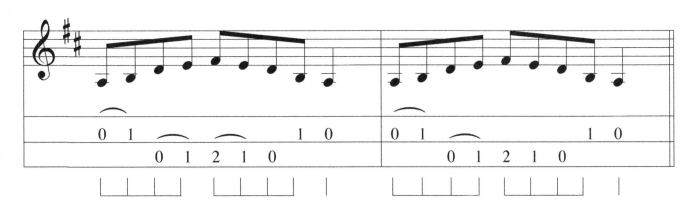

B.

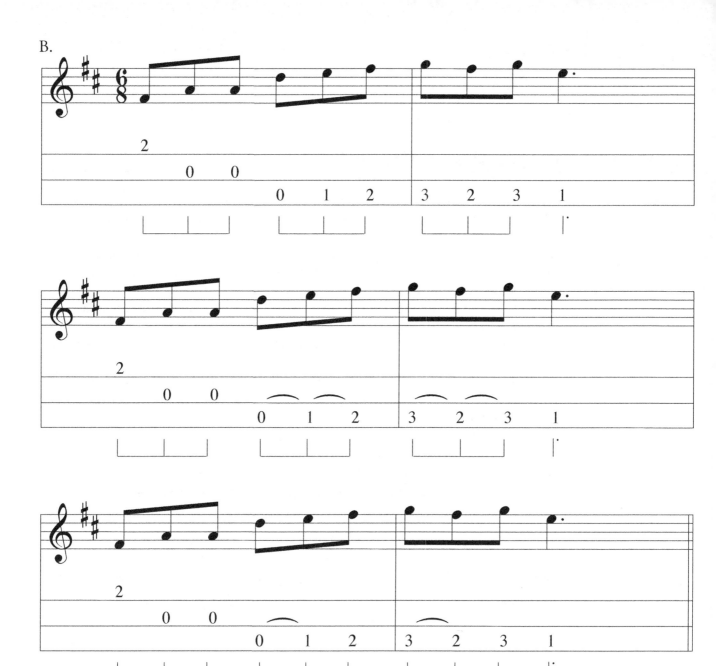

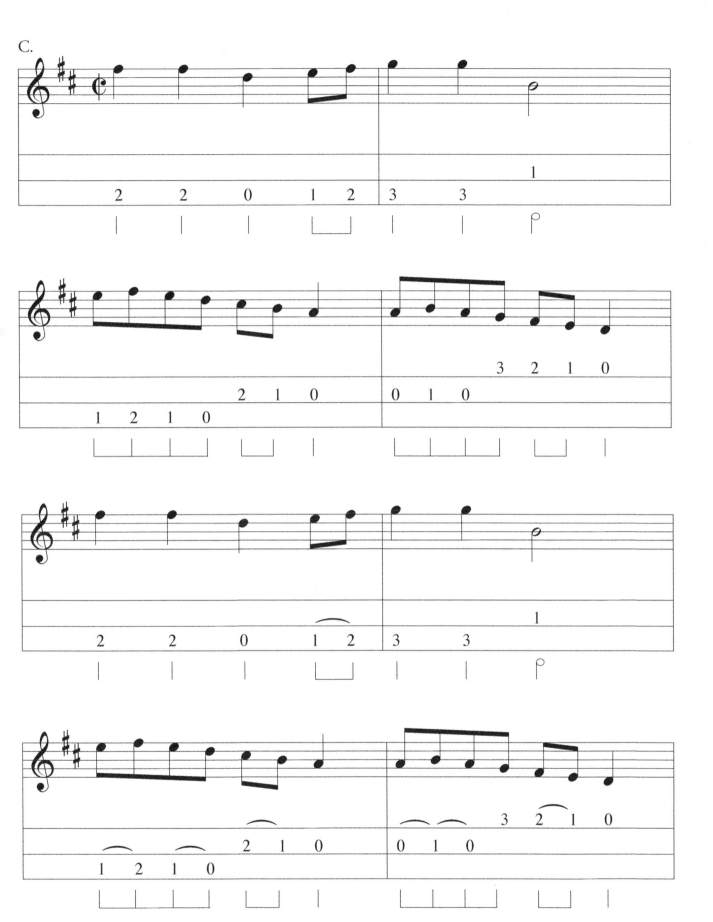

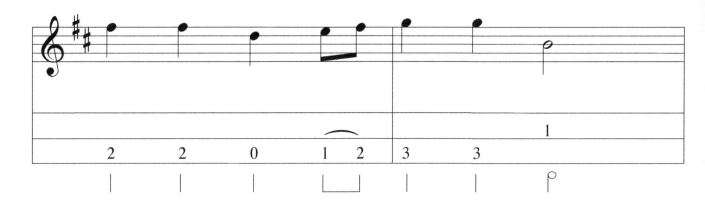

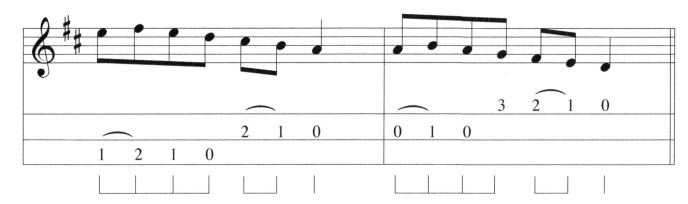

D. Combining slides with hammers and pulls

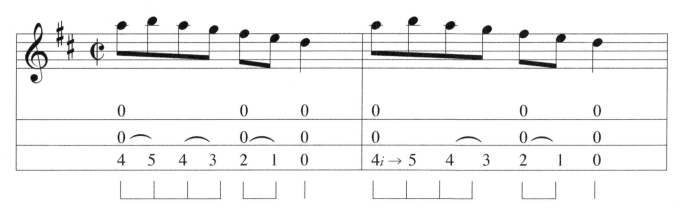

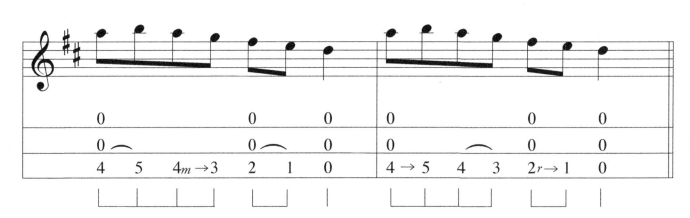

# ARPEGGIOS AND CHORDS

An arpeggio is a broken chord, that is, a chord whose notes are played one after another instead of together. Usually arpeggios begin with the lowest note and end with the highest. A chord is a group of three or more notes sounded at the same time. Our chord palette on the dulcimer is more limited than other instruments because of the diatonic scale and the fact that we typically only use three strings. Often dulcimer players use two note groupings that function as specific chords within a piece of music. The "chord" may be lacking a note or two but the ear still hears it as that chord in the context of the notes and chords around it.

Below are exercises that explore arpeggios and chords while offering challenges for left hand fingering, right hand flatpicking and playing slurs.

# Exercise #49: Easy Arpeggio Exercise

*(See page 106 for Helpful Hints.)*

A.

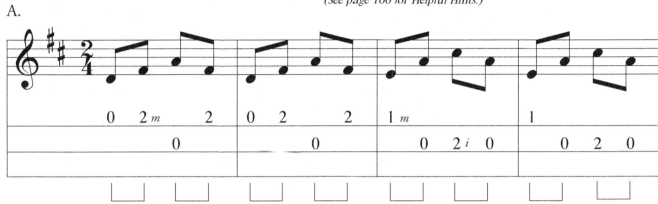

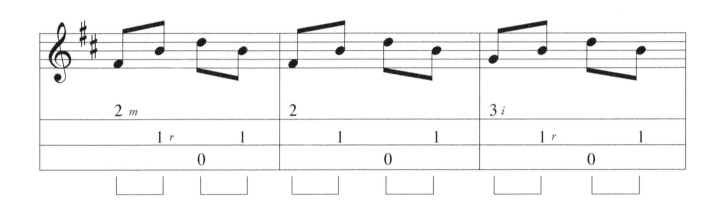

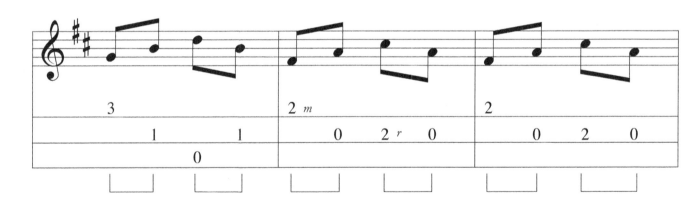

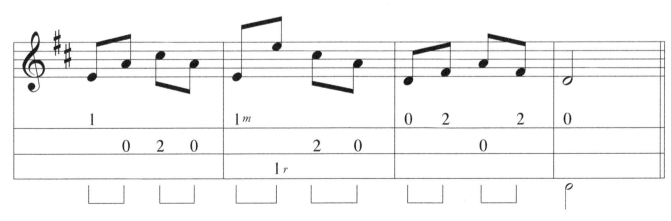

B. With Slurs

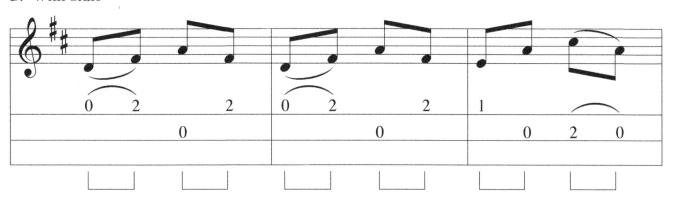

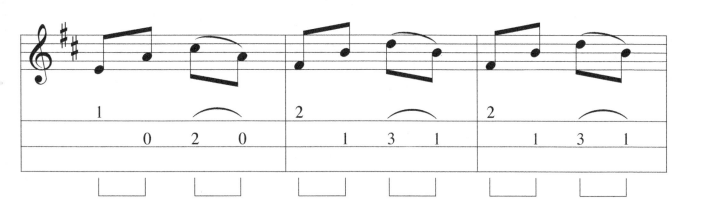

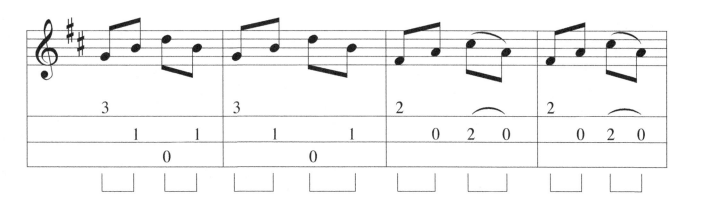

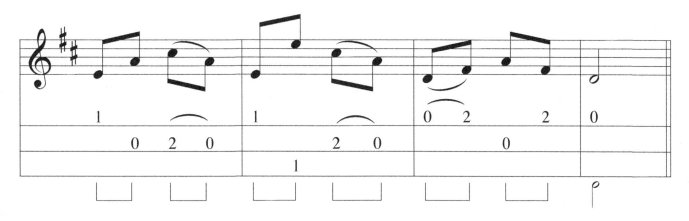

# Exercise #50: Lower Octave Arpeggio Study

*(See page 106 for Helpful Hints.)*

A.

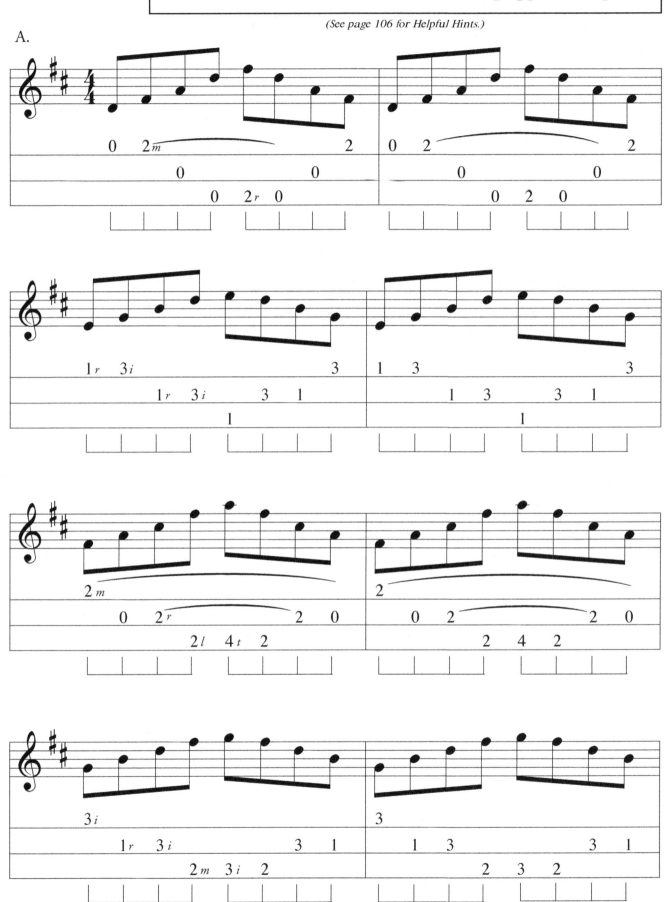

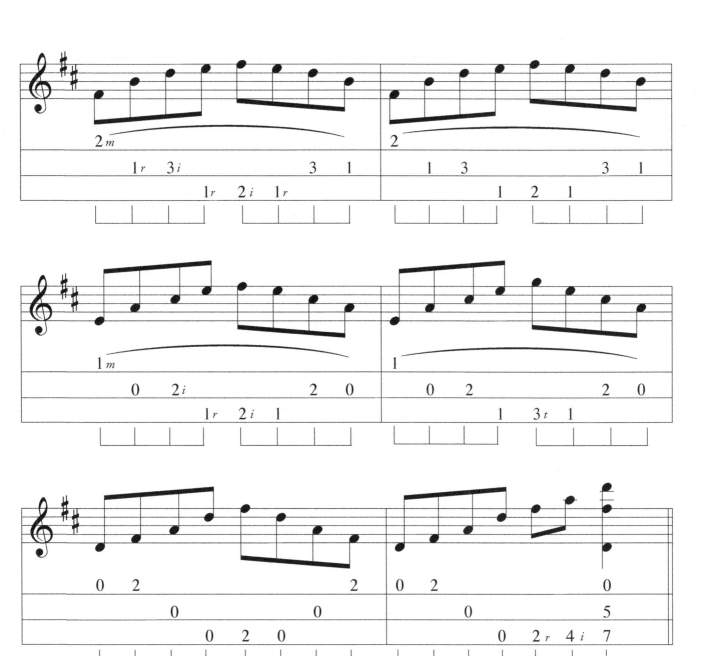

B. With slurs.

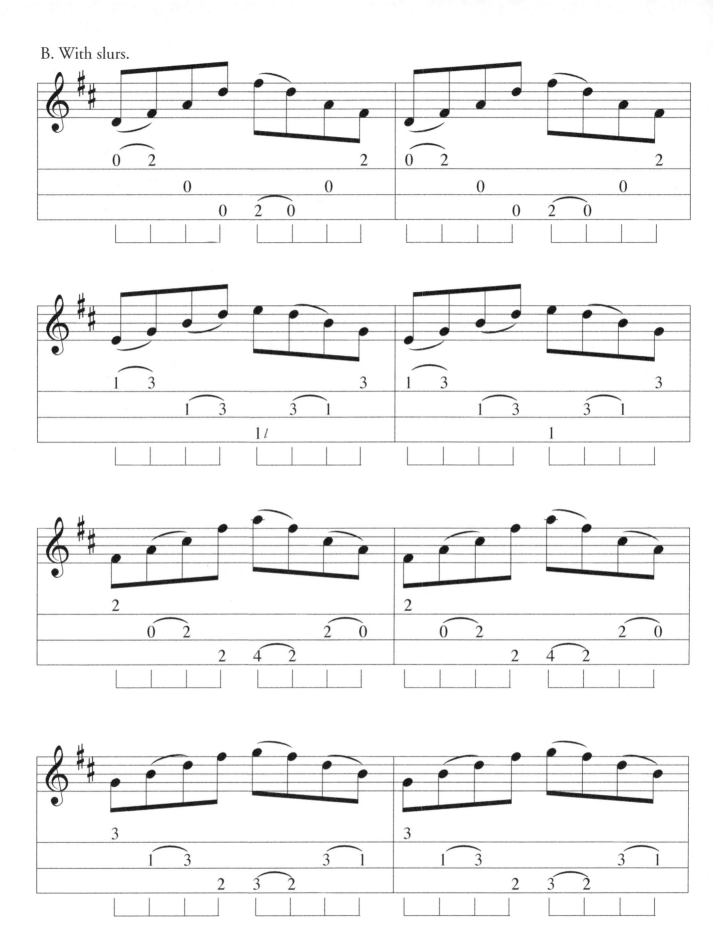

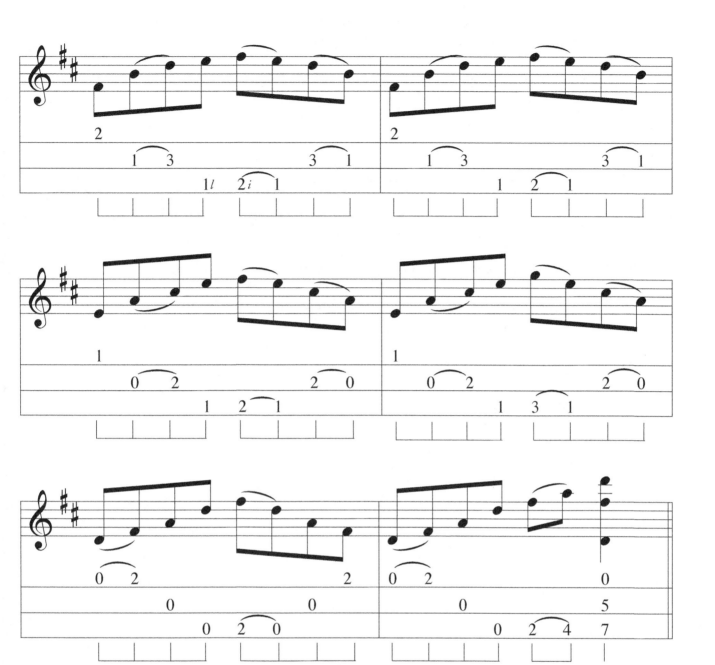

105

<table>
<tr><td>

*Helpful Hints
for
Exercise #49*

</td><td>

- The middle finger of the left hand acts as a guide finger for most of this exercise, staying on the bass string. Left hand fingering for B is the same as A.

- This exercise can either be flatpicked or fingerpicked.

</td></tr>
</table>

<table>
<tr><td>

*Helpful Hints
for
Exercise #50*

</td><td>

- Hold bass and middle string notes as much as possible. In measure 7 the ring finger on the middle string can act as a guide finger and remain in position. In measure 11, placc the middle finger on the bass and ring finger on the melody string and leave them in position.

</td></tr>
</table>

- This exercise can be done either flatpicking or fingerpicking.

- Try this exercise with a capo on fret 3 to shorten the left hand stretches.

106

# Exercise #51: Scale in Chords

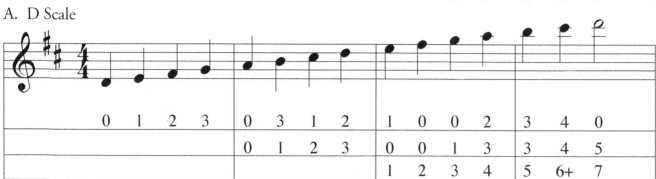

A. D Scale

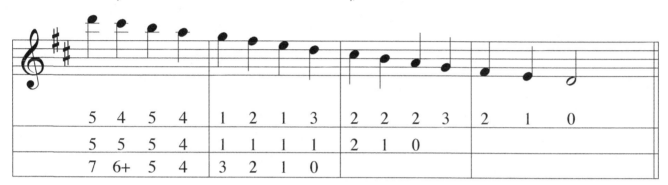

B. G Scale

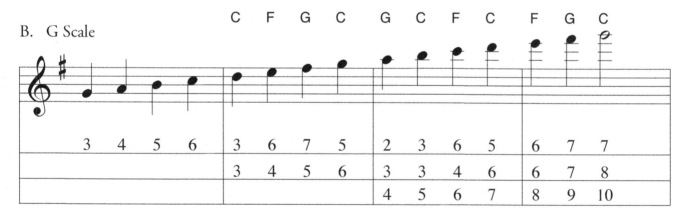

- This exercise presents one, of many, ways to harmonize a major scale. This version uses major chords ascending and mostly minor chords descending. I have named each chord, or two note grouping functioning as a chord, above the tab.

# Exercise #52: Flatpicking and Chord Exercise

109

## Exercise #53: D Major Scale Chord Exercise

■ To work further with alternating flatpicked notes and chords, try Tunes #1-4 in Section Eight.

*Helpful Hints*
*for*
*Exercise #52*
*& 53*

# DYNAMICS AND TONE

**Playing Loud & Soft**

The term dynamics refers to the gradations of loudness or softness with which a musical piece is performed. The dulcimer has a limited dynamic range, operating on the quieter end of the loud-soft continuum. Any variation in loudness can help a piece sound less "all the same." Below are some of the common dynamic markings used in classical music.

| Term | Meaning |
|------|---------|
| pianissimo | very soft |
| piano | soft |
| mezzo piano | moderately soft |
| mezzo forte | moderately loud |
| forte | loud |
| fortissimo | very loud |
| forte piano | loud, then soft |
| sfozando, sforzato | sharply accented |
| forzando, forzato | sharply accented |
| crescendo | gradually louder |
| decrescendo | gradually softer |
| diminuendo | gradually softer |

On the dulcimer, the right hand is responsible for varying the dynamic level of a musical passage. To play louder the right hand (with pick or fingers) strikes the strings harder; to play softer the picking is more gentle. Imagine refining the art of varying dynamic level to the point where you can distinguish between a passage played soft versus moderately soft. Or moderately soft versus moderately loud.

Most of the exercises in this book can usefully be played with varying loudness and softness. This helps both in learning to vary dynamic level and in adding an extra measure of artistry to an exercise to help maintain interest. Varying loud and soft also builds strength and develops control in the right hand. Here are a few suggestions for working on dynamics.

**Loud/Soft Exercises**

• Using Exercise 3, play one section loud, then repeat soft. Then, play loud on one string, soft on the next, etc. Play the 4's as loud as you can, then as soft as you can.

• Play one part of Exercise 14 over and over, gradually becoming louder then steadily becoming quiet.

• Take the two octave scale in D in Exercise 20A, start loud but get softer as the scale rises, then move from quiet to loud as the scale descends. Remember that the left hand plays no role in varying dynamic level. Do not press harder with the left hand when playing louder!

• In Exercise 24F, play a measure of sixteenth notes loud followed by a measure of eighth notes quiet. Then, reverse. Then, play a few measures moderately loud followed by a few moderately soft.

• Locate your own personal dynamic range on the dulcimer. How loudly can you play? How soft? How many levels of sound can you find between loud and soft?

One meaning of the word tone is the quality of sound. An instrument is said to have good tone if it has good intonation (for dulcimers, properly fretted and tuned) and pleasing tone color (a blend of harmonic overtones defined as pleasing). The tone produced by an instrument depends not only on the details of its construction, but also on the player. On the dulcimer, the thickness and material of a flatpick can have great effect on the quality of tone coming from the instrument. For example, a thicker pick may produce a deeper and richer tone but then this is not necessarily appropriate for all types of music. Dulcimer players can also achieve different tone colors by varying where they strike the strings with their right hand. Playing closer to the bridge produces a harsher, more nasal sound. Playing closer to the frets gives a mellower, sweeter tone. To practice achieving different tone colors use the exercises suggested above for working on dynamics. Add another variable – while varying loud and soft also change the tone color.

# Tone Color

# CROSSING STRINGS AND FINGERS

Below are three additional exercises that focus both on crossing strings and left hand fingerings.

## Exercise #54: The Spider

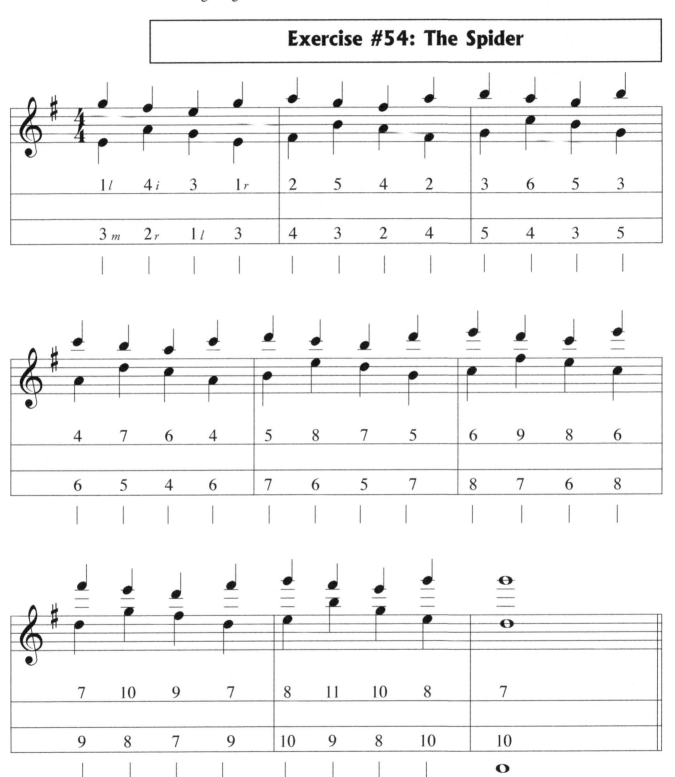

| | |
| --- | --- |
| *Helpful Hints for Exercise #54* | ■ This exercise is fingerpicked. Left hand fingerings are important and remain the same for the entire exercise as notated in the first measure. The fingerings have every finger (except the thumb) on the bass and on the melody string in each measure. |

# Exercise #55: The Climbing Spider

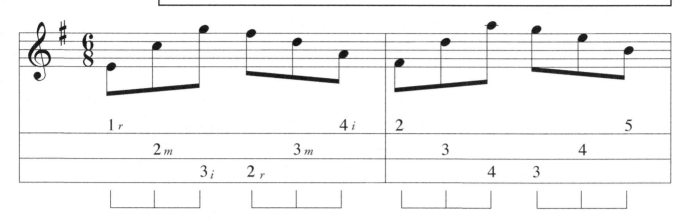

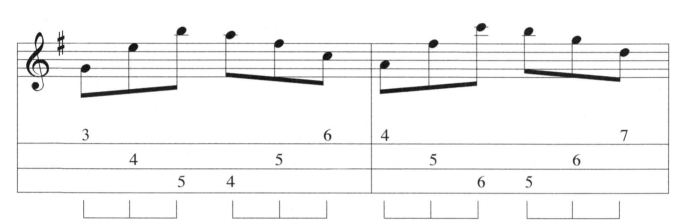

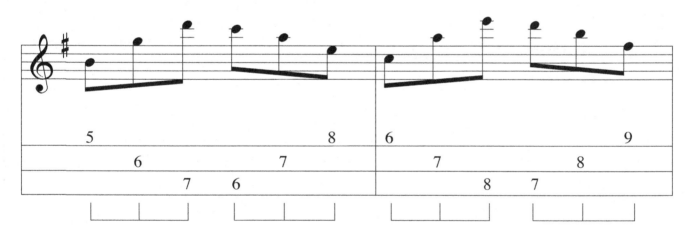

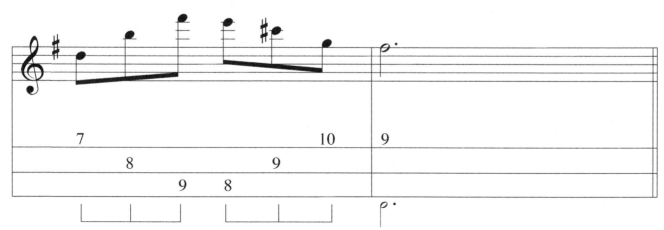

■ This exercise can be played either fingerpicked or flatpicked. Left hand fingering is the same for the entire exercise as notated in the first measure.

# Exercise #56: Crossing Strings Blues

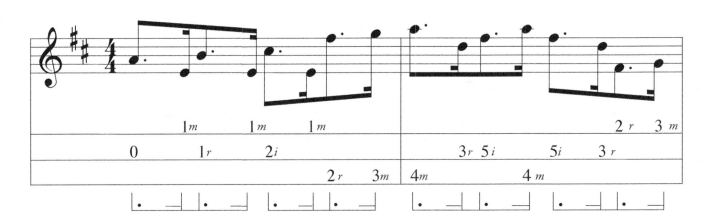

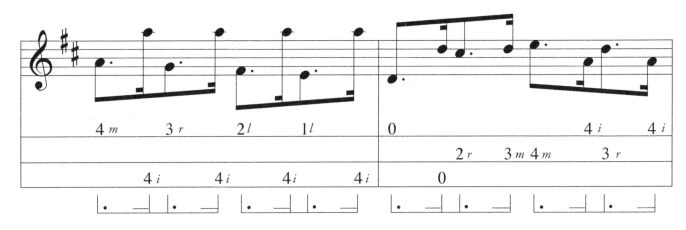

*Helpful Hints for Exercise #56*

- This exercise features dotted eighth notes followed by sixteenths that give it a lilt or swing, rather than a straight rhythm.

- Alternate the pick back and forth with a different direction for each note.

- Keep left hand fingers in place as much as possible. For example, in measure 1 the middle finger stays on the first fret of the bass string until the last beat. In measure 2, the middle finger remains on the fourth fret of the melody string for the first three beats.

*This page has been
left blank to avoid
awkward page turns.*

# SEVEN

## Adding Strings

Most dulcimers have three strings but it is not uncommon these days to find four- and even five-string instruments. Four-string dulcimers that include a doubled melody string essentially function like three-string instruments. All of the exercises in the first six sections of this book work for this arrangement since the two strings of the doubled melody string are fingered or noted together as if they were one string. But, if you have a dulcimer with four or five equally spaced strings (also known as equi-distant strings), this chapter will help you explore the additional possibilities that the added strings present.

## FOUR STRINGS

Following are two right hand exercises for a four-string dulcimer in any tuning. I am labeling the four strings this way: the string closest to you as the dulcimer sits on your lap is the melody string, the next string in is melody 2, the next string is the middle string, and the string farthest from you is the bass string.

### Exercise #57: Flatpicking Patterns for Four Strings

A. Alternate Strings   B.            C.            D.

| 0 | | | | | | 0 | 0 0 | | | | 0 0 |
|---|---|---|---|---|---|---|---|---|---|---|---|
| | 0 | | | 0 | | | 0 0 | | 0 | | |
| 0 | | | 0 | | | 0 | | | | 0 | |
| | | 0 | 0 | | | | | 0 | 0 0 | | |

E.            F.            G. Outer-Inner   H.

| 0 0 | | | 0 0 | | | 0 | | | 0 | |
|---|---|---|---|---|---|---|---|---|---|---|
| | 0 | 0 | | 0 | 0 | | 0 | | | 0 |
| 0 | | 0 | | 0 | 0 | | 0 | | 0 | |
| | 0 0 | | | 0 0 | | | 0 | | 0 | |

119

I.               J.            K. Inner-Outer        L.

```
      0                        0                          0                            0
           0                        0                  0                        0
         0                        0                              0               0
       0                        0                                  0           0
```

M.               N.             O.             P.

```
                   0                   0               0                              0
         0                   0                   0                       0
      0               0                                         0         0
         0                        0                        0         0
```

*Helpful Hints*
*for*
*Exercise #57*

- This exercise is very similar to Exercise 14 but expanded to incorporate four equi-distant strings. Review the helpful hints for Exercise 14.

## Exercise #58: Fingerpicking Patterns for Four Strings

A.               B.             C.             D.

E.               F.             G.             H.

I.               J.             K.             L.

M.               N.             O.             P.

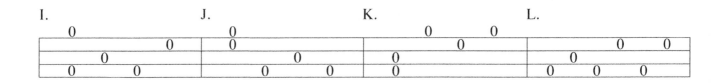

Q.

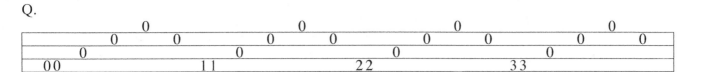

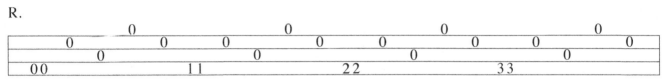

R.

[Complete as in Q above]

S.

[Complete as in Q above]

*Helpful Hints for Exercise #58*

- Fingering for the right hand for all of these exercises: Thumb plays the melody string (the string closest to you), index plays the next string in (melody2 ), middle plays the middle string, ring plays the bass string.

# CROSS STRING PLAYING

Probably the most common four-string equi-distant tuning is D-A-D-D, which has the two strings closest to the player tuned to the same pitch, one octave above the bass string. Having two strings tuned the same makes possible a technique that I call cross-string playing. By alternating between the two strings to play a melody while leaving fingers down as long as possible, a smooth, ringing and legato sound can be obtained that imitates the free-ringing strings of a harp. I've heard this style of playing called Harris picking, evidently named after its originator on the dulcimer Rodger Harris, but the basic idea of crossing between strings to find adjacent melody notes has also been used on guitar, banjo and other stringed instruments for many years.

The first exercise below gives some of the basic chords in the D-A-D-D tuning, while the second begins exploring cross-string playing with a few scales. Following are two exercises that focus on playing melodies in this style.

## Exercise #59: Basic Chords in D-A-D-D

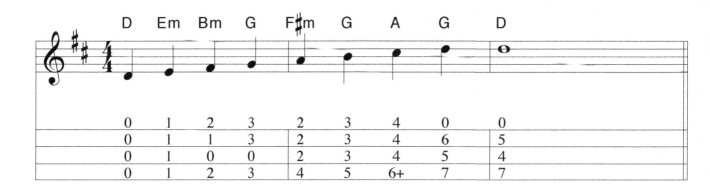

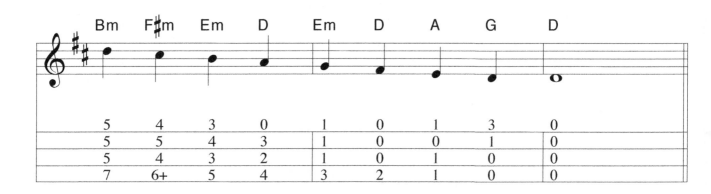

# Exercise #60: Cross-String Scales in D-A-D-D

A. Basic D Major Scale (Ascending)                    (Descending)

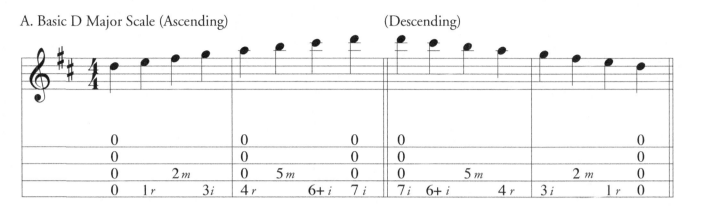

B. Alternate D Major Scale (Ascending)                 (Descending)

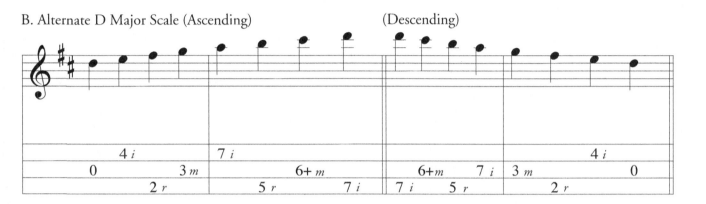

C.  G Major Scale

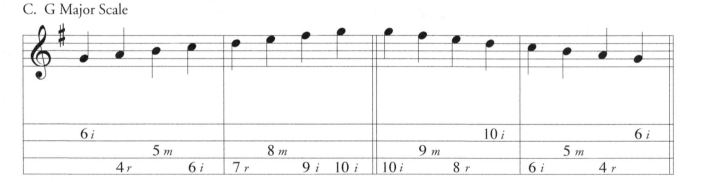

<table>
<tr><td rowspan="4">Helpful Hints<br>for<br>Exercise #60</td></tr>
</table>

| *Helpful Hints for Exercise #60* | ▪ Hold notes as long as possible--keep fingers in place until you have to move to another note. Let one note sustain into the next. |
| --- | --- |

▪ Hold notes as long as possible--keep fingers in place until you have to move to another note. Let one note sustain into the next.

▪ In 60B keep fingers down as you place them until the end of the first measure, then shift this chord formation up the neck with the index leading the way to fret 7.

▪ Start 60C with three fingers down on frets 6, 4 and 5.

# Exercise #61: Chimes I

Tuning: D - A - D - D

A.

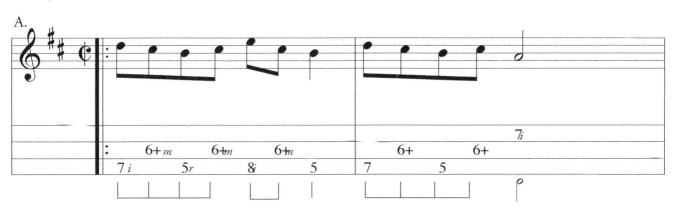

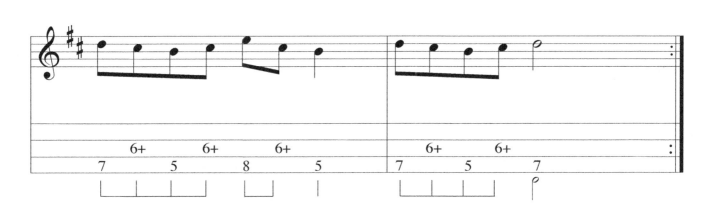

B.

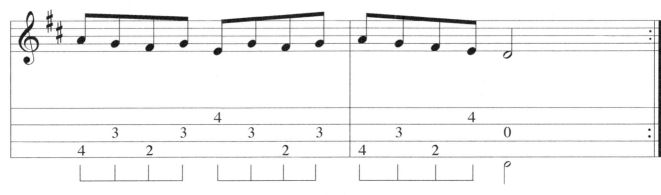

Helpful Hints
for
Exercise #61

- Remember to alternate the direction of the pick with each note to keep the sound as smooth and legato as possible.

- In 61A the starting left hand position is the index finger on fret 7 of the melody string, middle on fret 6+ of melody2 with ring also on fret 5 of the melody. The ring and middle fingers stay in position for the entire exercise. Only the index moves.

- In 61B the starting left hand position is index on fret 4 of the melody, ring on fret 2 of the melody behind the index, and middle on fret 3 of melody2. Again, the ring and middle fingers remain in place for the entire exercise.

# Exercise #62: Chimes II

Tuning: D - A - D -D

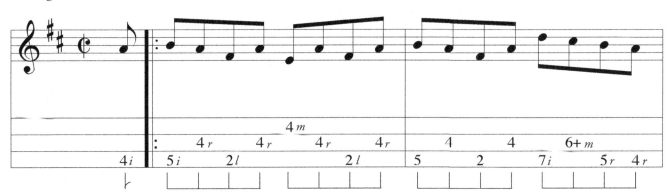

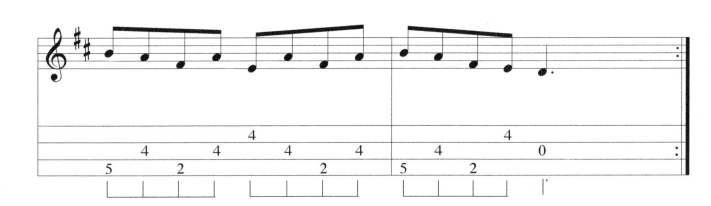

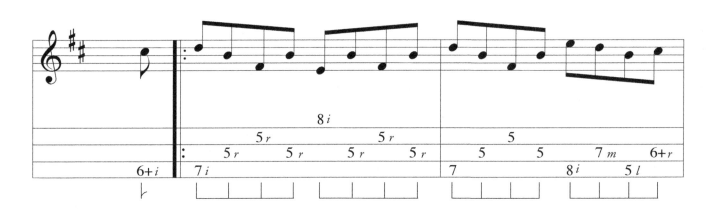

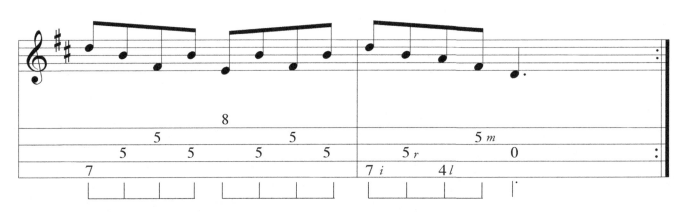

- Slide the index finger from fret 4 to 5 to start, then place in position the little finger on fret 2 of the melody string, ring on fret 4 on melody2, and middle on fret 4 of the middle string. Leave these fingers in place until the index moves up to fret 7.

- To practice cross-string playing in a piece of music try Tune 13, The Ash Grove.

# FIVE STRINGS

In 1994 I began playing a five-string dulcimer built for me by Blue Lion in Santa Margarita, CA. Because a number of other players are now exploring the five-string, I've included a few exercises using this stringing arrangement. The five-string tuning for these exercises is D-A-D-A-D. This is the same as the standard D-A-D tuning but with two lower-pitched strings tuned to an "A" and a "D" below the lowest string in D-A-D. This gives the instrument a range that extends a full octave below a standard dulcimer, encompassing both the "bass" dulcimer and a "normal" dulcimer in one instrument. This allows greater flexibility in arranging tunes and songs by making it possible to play melodies an octave lower than usual. It also expands the palette of chords available to harmonize these melodies, and enables the creation of dulcimer chords anchored by true bass notes.

Following are four exercises for the five-string dulcimer: one for the right hand, two for the left, and then an arrangement of a simple, familiar tune that explores the capabilities of the instrument.

A.

B.

C.

D.

E.

F.

G.

H.

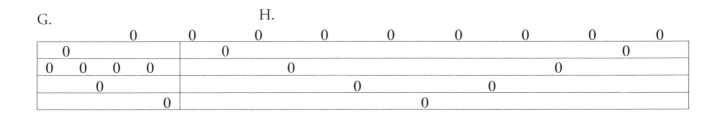

**I.**

```
            0
      0           0
    0                 0
  0                       0
0   0   0   0   0   0   0   0
```

**J.**

```
              0               0
        0           0
0   0   0
                        0
```

**K.**

```
        0           0
      0       0
            0
0               0
    0
```

**L.**

```
          0
        0               0
                  0
            0               0
                  0               0
```

---

## Exercise #64: Five-String Lower Octave Scales

Tuning: D - A - D - A - D

A. D Major Scale

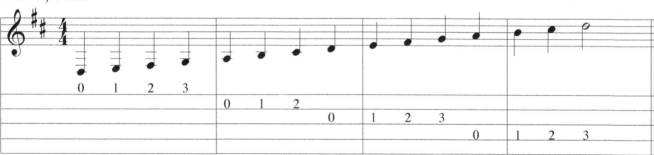

```
0   1   2   3
              0   1   2
                        0   1   2   3
                                  0   1   2   3
```

B. G Major Scale

```
3   4   5   6
              3   4   5   6
                        4   5   6
                                  3   4   5   6
```

# Exercise #65: Basic Five-String Chords

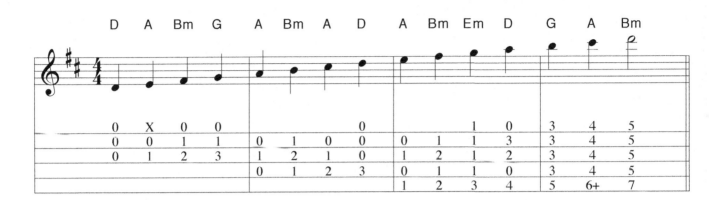

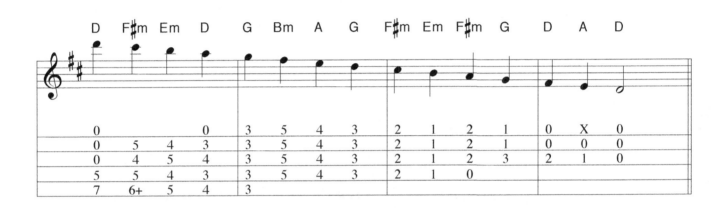

# Exercise #66: Exploring the Five-String Dulcimer

Tuning: D - A - D - A - D

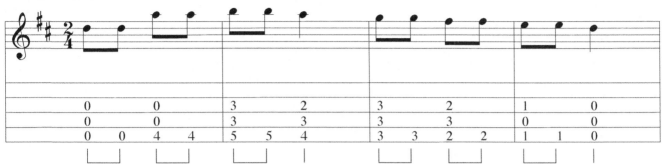

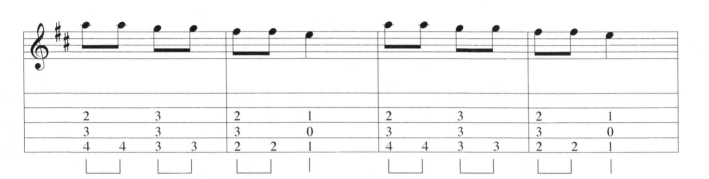

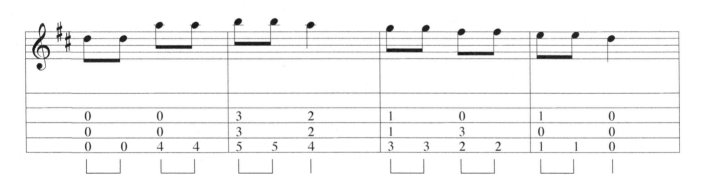

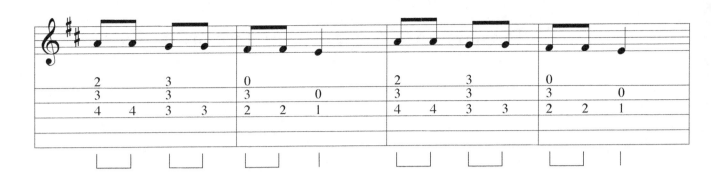

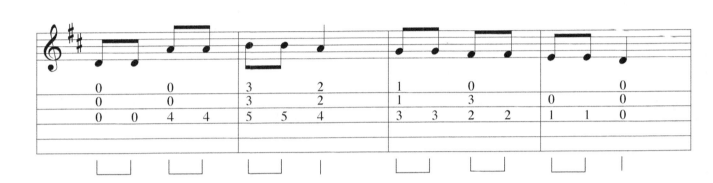

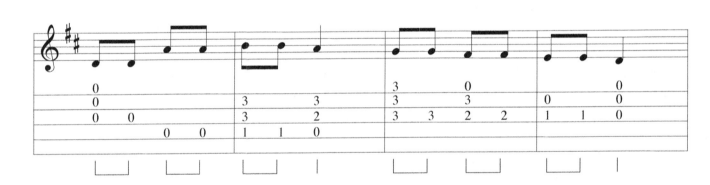

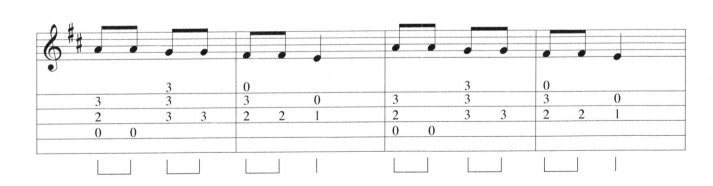

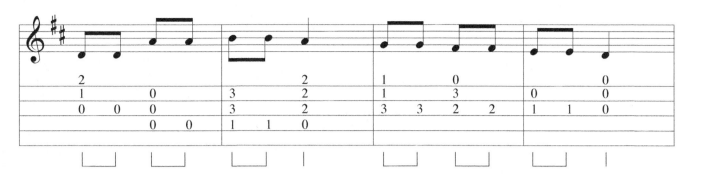

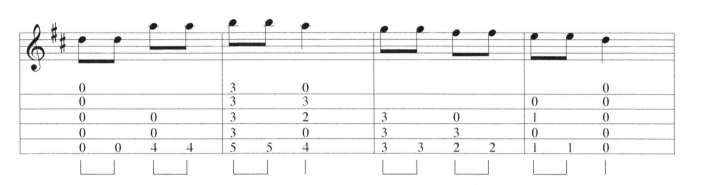

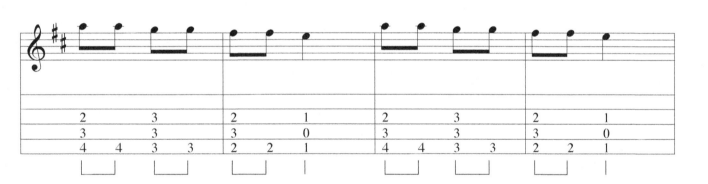

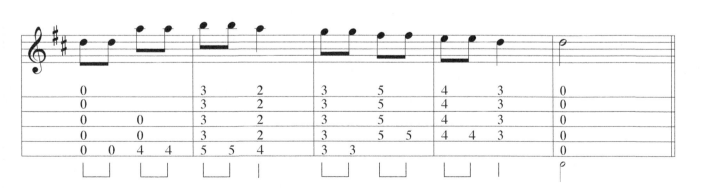

■ This arrangement of Twinkle, Twinkle Little Star has four parts: the first time through is a standard D-A-D arrangement. The second repetition is basically the same arrangement but played an octave lower. The third is in the same octave as #2 but stays within frets 1-3 by crossing to higher-pitched strings. The fourth time the melody is back to the melody string but uses the two lower bass strings to create bigger chords in some places.

For further work with the five-string, try Tunes 14 and 15, The South Wind and Grace Nugent, in Section Eight.

More arrangements for four- and five-string dulcimer can be found in my book *The Pleasures of Hope*, also published by Mel Bay.

# EIGHT

## A Few Good Tunes...

This section offers a few tunes that illustrate some of the right and left-hand techniques explored in the exercises and studies in previous sections. Here is a chance to practice some of these techniques with an actual piece of music.

Helpful Hints for each tune start on page 169.

# Tune #1: The First Noel

Tuning: D - A - D

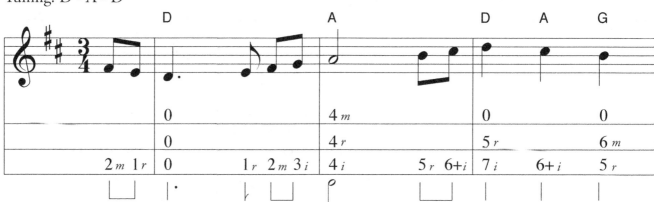

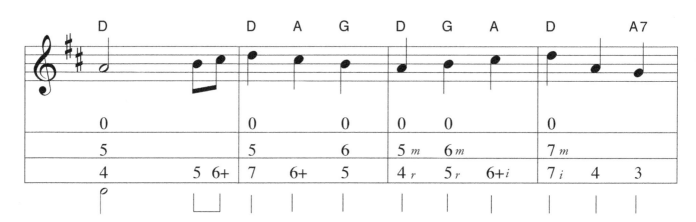

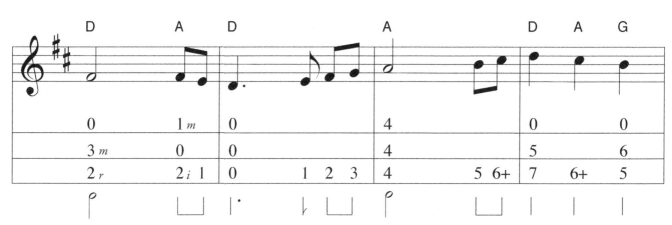

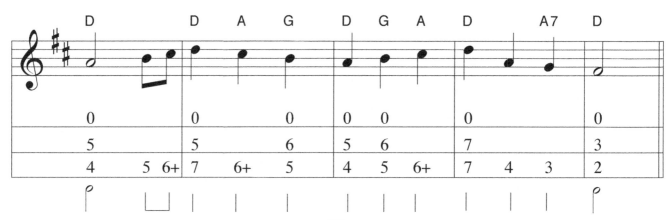

REFRAIN:

* Variation: Measure 3 - 4 of the refrain

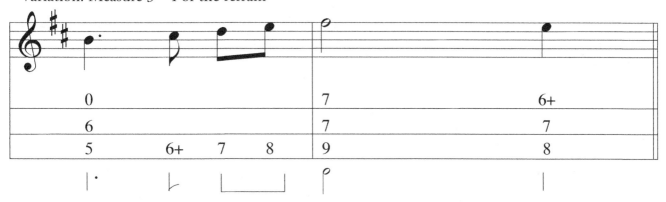

** Variation: Measure 6 - 8 of the refrain

# Tune #2: The South Wind (Easiest Version)

Tuning: D - A - D
Capo 3

138

# Tune #3: Loch Lomond

Tuning: D - A - D

* Variation

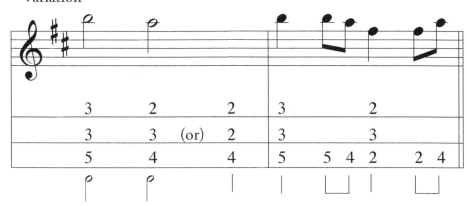

Tuning: D - A - D

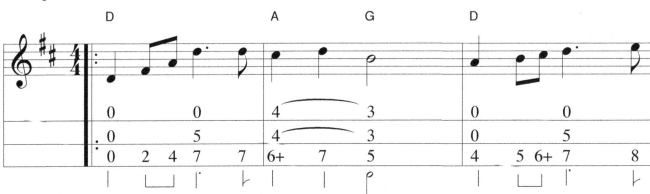

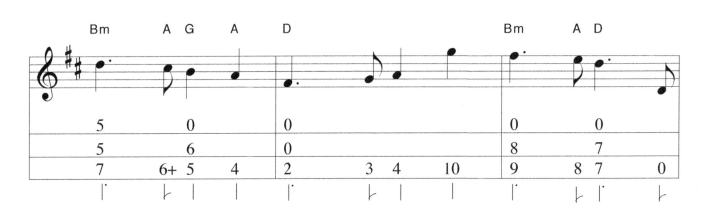

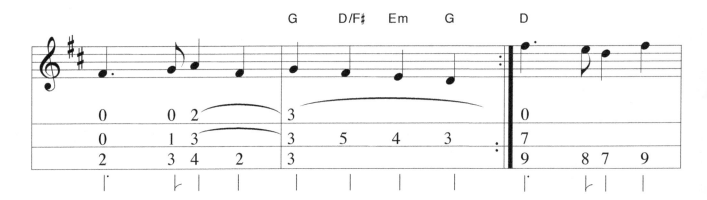

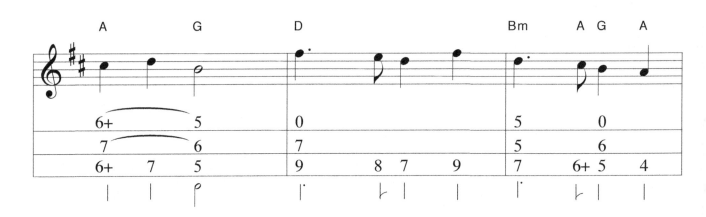

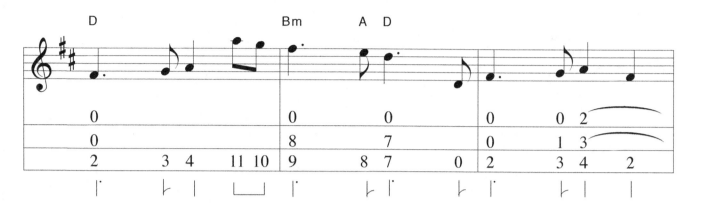
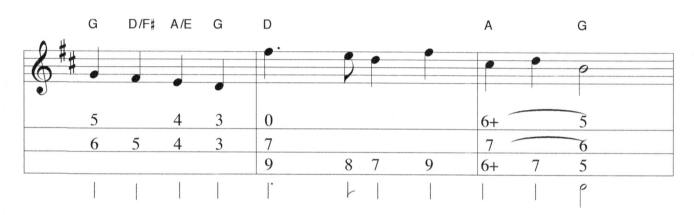
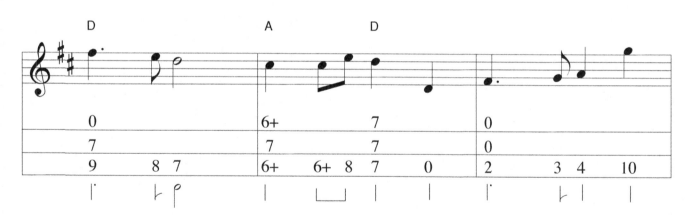
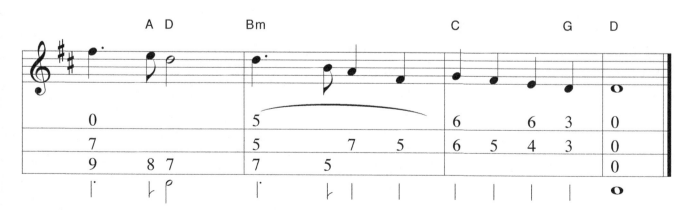

# Tune #5: Old Molly Hare

Tuning: D - A - D

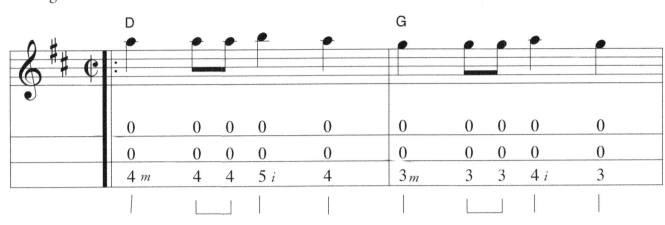

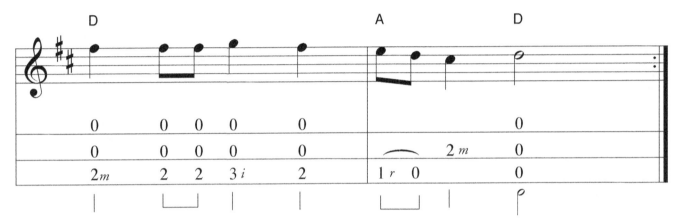

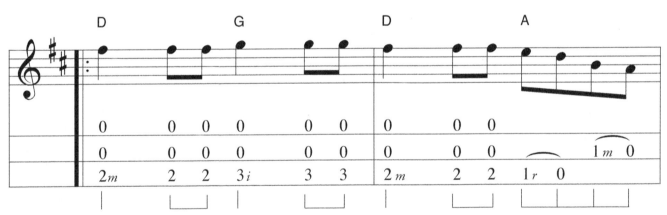

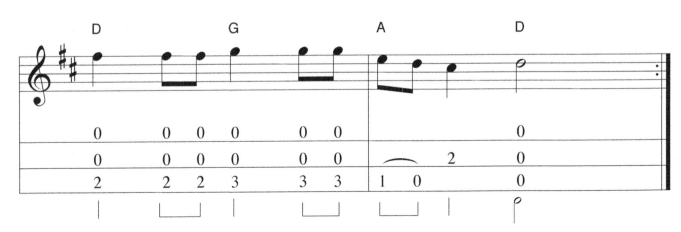

Tuning: D - A - D

Tuning: D - A - D

→ = *Slide*

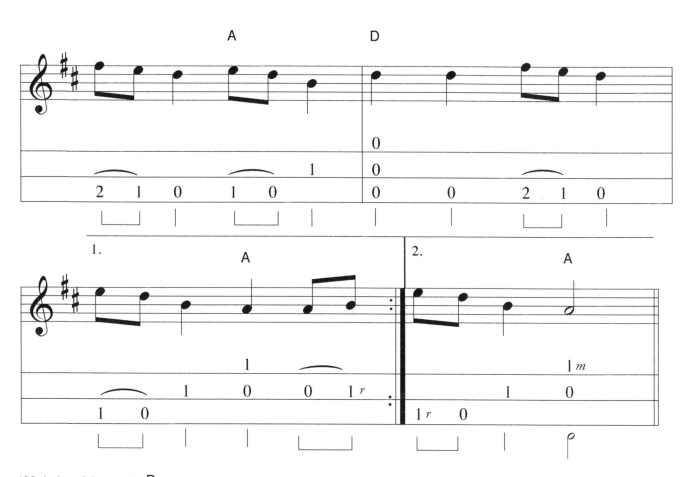

*Variation: Measure 9  D

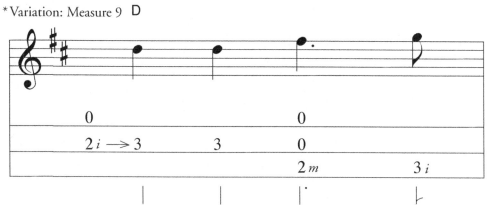

# Tune #7: Sally in the Garden

D - A - C Tuning

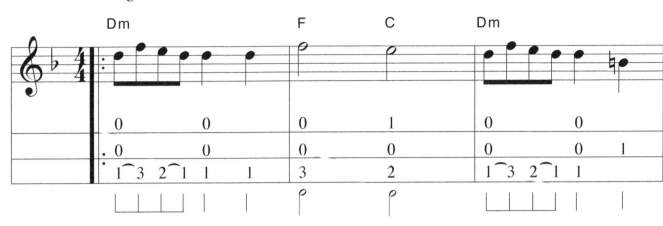

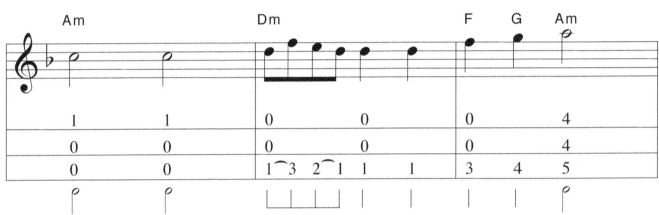

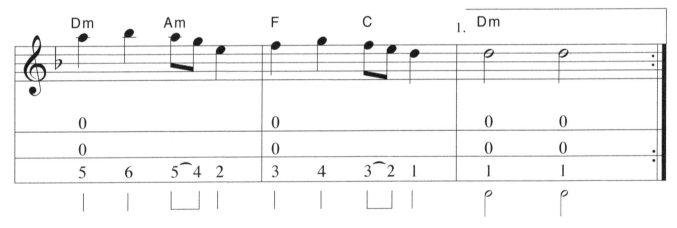

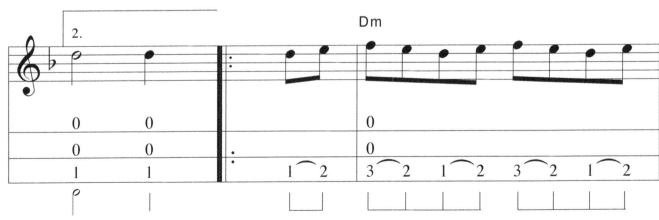

148

# Tune #8: The South Wind (Fingerpicking Version)

Tuning: D - A - D
Capo 3

# Tune #9: Megan's Daughter

Tuning: D - A - D

# Tune #10: The Munster Buttermilk

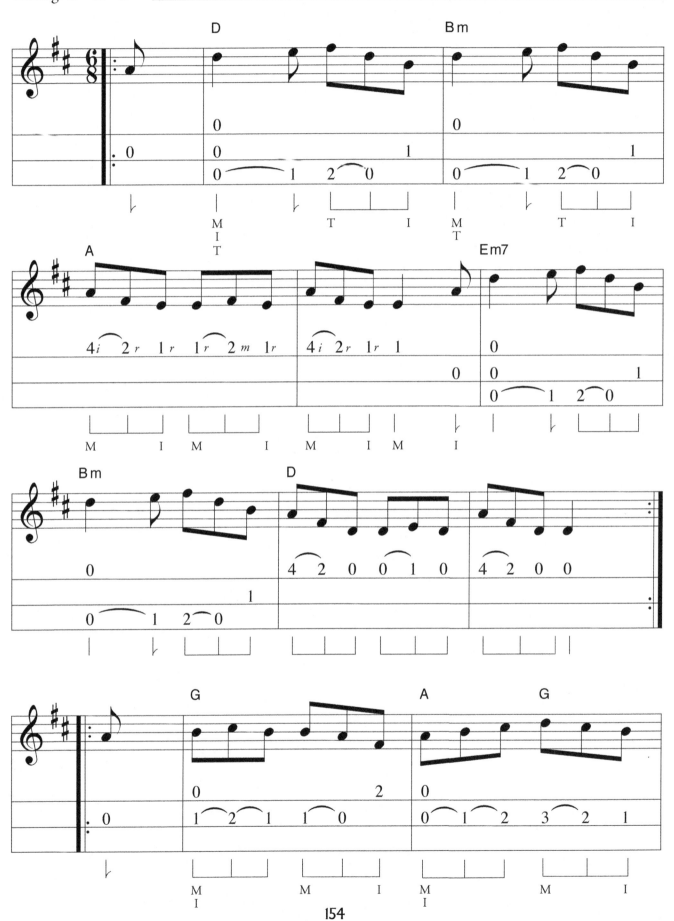

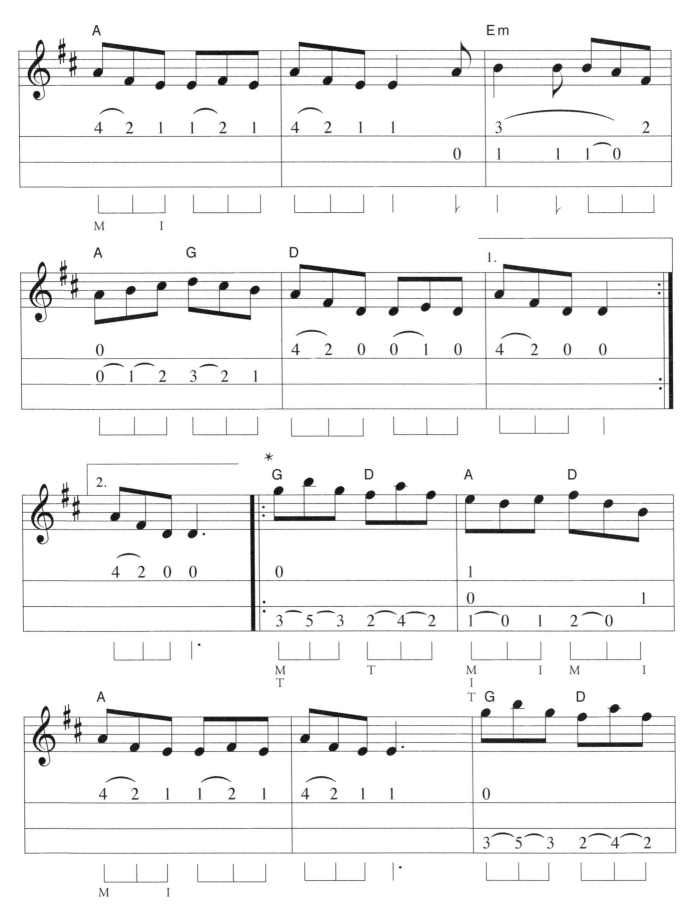

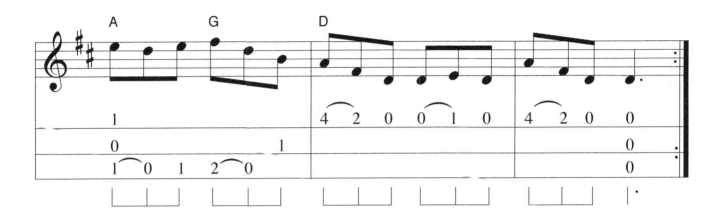

\* Variation

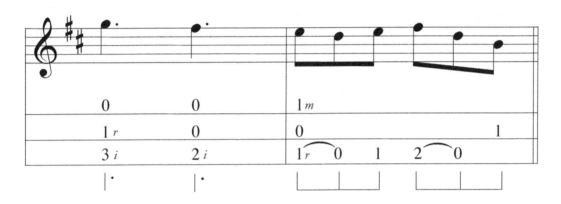

*This page has been
left blank to avoid
awkward page turns.*

# Tune #11: The Scotch Cap

Tuning: D - A - D

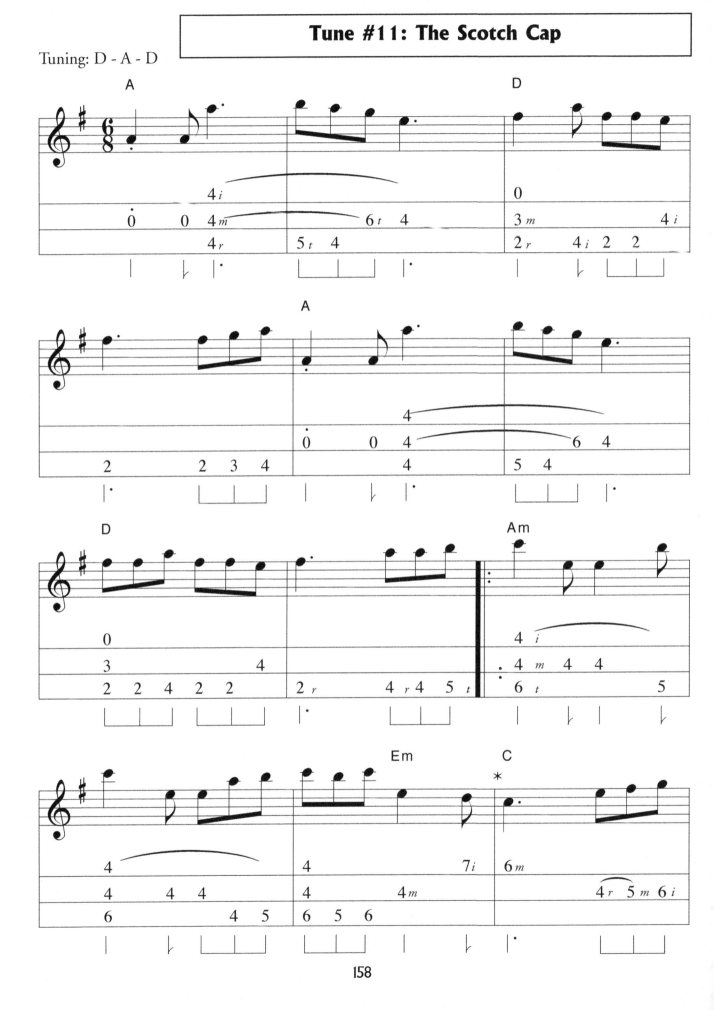

158

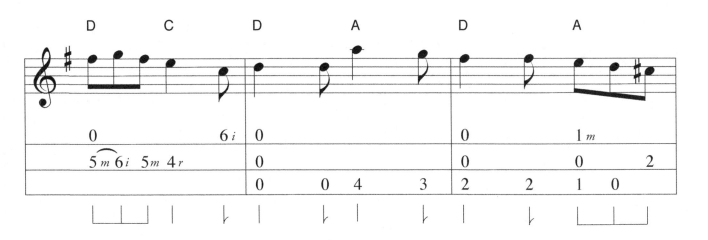

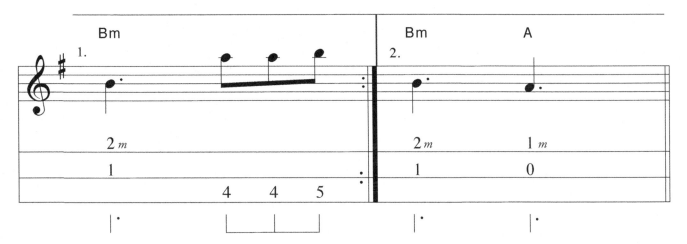

* Variation

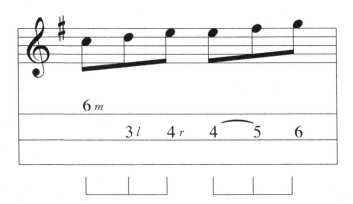

# Tune #12: Harvest Home

Tuning: D - A - D

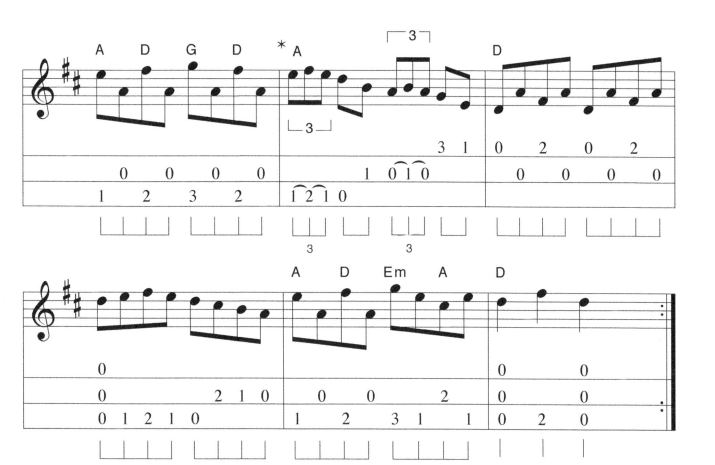

* Variation

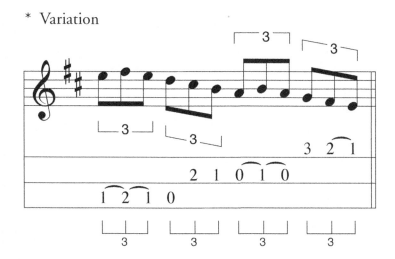

161

Tuning: D - A - D - D
Capo 3

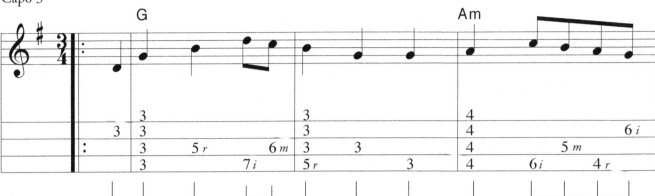

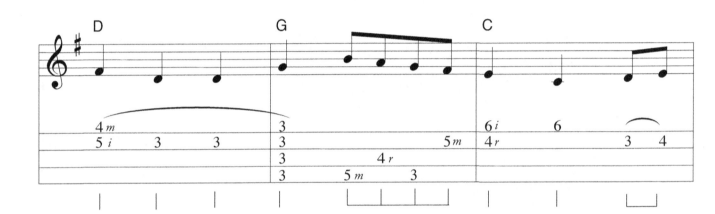

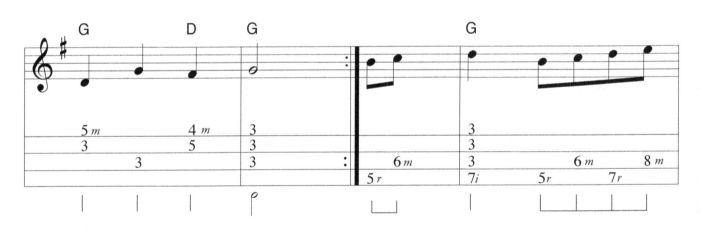

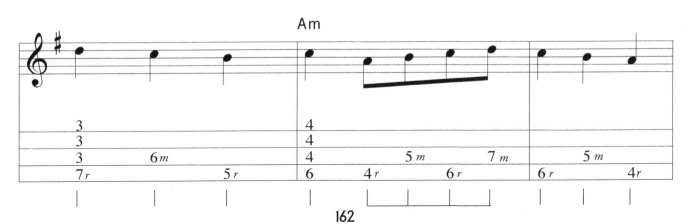

Tuning: D - A - D - A - D
Capo 3

# Tune #15: Grace Nugent

Tuning: D - A - D - A - D
Capo 4

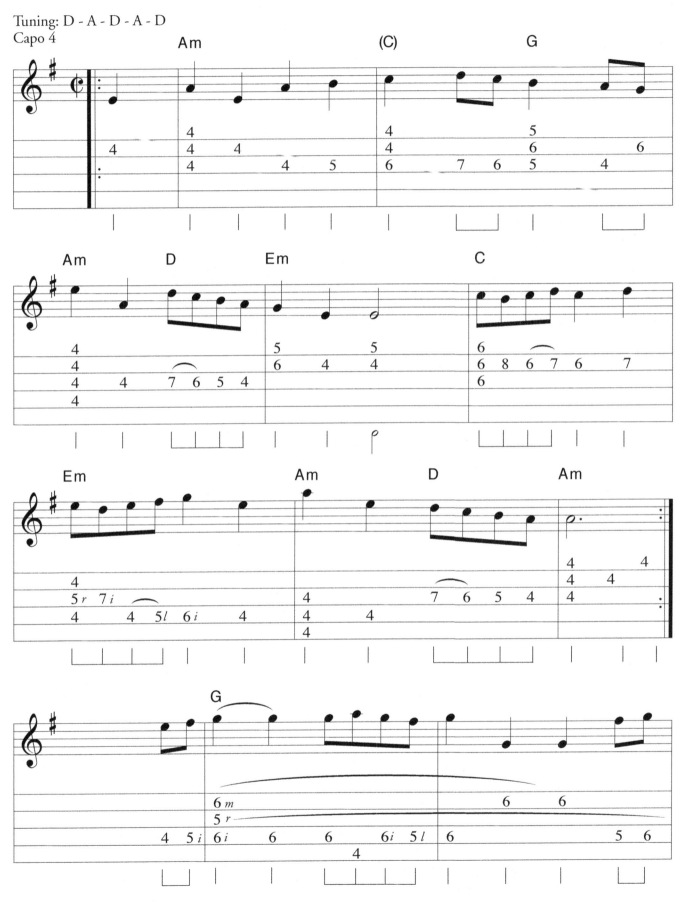

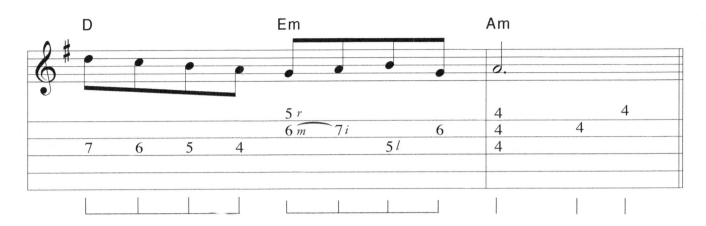

* Variation

<table>
<tr>
<td>

*Helpful Hints for Tune #1*

</td>
<td>

- The First Noel provides an opportunity to both practice chords and to try alternating individual flatpicked notes with chords as in Exercises 6, 52 and 53.

</td>
</tr>
<tr>
<td>

*Helpful Hints for Tune #2*

</td>
<td>

- The second part of The South Wind is fingered especially for players who use their thumbs. Non-thumb players could use the index finger in place of the thumb and ring finger instead of the middle.

- The finger on the middle string acts as a guide finger in the second part, staying in place through the first three measures.

- Remember that fret numbers notated with the capo are actual fret numbers, since the notes themselves do not change with the presence of the capo. Therefore, fret 3 equals the capo (which is placed at the third fret), fret 4 is actually the 4th fret on the instrument regardless of whether the capo is there, etc.

</td>
</tr>
<tr>
<td>

*Helpful Hints for Tune #3*

</td>
<td>

- Loch Lomond illustrates the use of guide and pivot fingers as discussed in Section Four and demonstrated in Exercise 21.

- In the last note of the first full measure, the middle finger on fret 1 acts as a pivot finger. It remains in place while the index pivots from the melody string to the first fret of the bass string. The index finger then becomes a guide finger, staying on the bass string while moving from fret 1 to fret 3 as the ring finger drops into position on the first fret of the middle string to form the G chord that follows.

- In measures 4-6, the ring finger acts as a guide, staying on the middle string as the melody moves around it.

</td>
</tr>
<tr>
<td>

*Helpful Hints for Tune #4*

</td>
<td>

- Tha Mi Tinn Leis A' Ghaol or The Languor of Love is a Scottish piece from the Simon Fraser Collection, first published in 1816. Sustain is very important to this piece so hold bass notes and chord tones as long as possible and pay attention to ties.

- In the seventh measure of the second part, after playing the 2-3-4 chord, slide whatever fingers you are using on the bass and middle strings up to fret 5 of the bass and fret 6 of the middle. These fingers act as guides.

- This piece also provides an opportunity to both practice chords and to try alternating individual flatpicked notes with chords as in Exercises 6, 52 and 53.

</td>
</tr>
</table>

<table>
<tr><td>

*Helpful Hints<br>for<br>Tune #5*

</td><td>

- Old Molly Hare is a good tune for working on keeping back fingers in place (See Exercises 4-6). Start with the middle finger on fret 4 of the melody string with the ring finger in place behind it on fret 3 of the melody. Reach up with the index to play fret 5, then move this entire formation down one fret so that the middle is on fret 3 with the ring in place behind it on fret 2. The middle and ring fingers do not leave the melody string. Continue moving in this way and when you arrive at the last measure of the first part, the ring finger is already in place to play fret 1 of the melody string.

- The second version of Old Molly Hare is full of hammer-ons and pull-offs. See Exercises 31-34 to work on these.

</td></tr>
</table>

<table>
<tr><td>

*Helpful Hints<br>for<br>Tune #6*

</td><td>

- The old time fiddle tune Shooting Creek contains several slides (see also Exercise 35) which are indicated by arrows. Note that the third slide in the piece, at the end of measure 6, takes up the rhythmic space of two eighth notes. This passage could be handled by a hammer-on as well as a slide. See Exercise 48 to explore different ways to articulate using slurs.

</td></tr>
</table>

<table>
<tr><td>

*Helpful Hints<br>for<br>Tune #7*

</td><td>

- Sally in the Garden provides another great opportunity to work on hammer-pull combinations. Refer back to Exercise 32C and D to practice these.

</td></tr>
</table>

<table>
<tr><td>

*Helpful Hints<br>for<br>Tune #8*

</td><td>

- See Tune 2, the easier version of The South Wind for possible left hand fingerings. This fingerpicked version is fingered for right hand brushes with both the index and middle fingers along with a few pinches. A brush has just one right hand finger notated while a pinch has two or more. See Exercise 38 to review brushes and pinches.

- This version is also good for alternating right hand fingers. See Exercises 39-45.

- The variation in the second half of the second part might be used only once, perhaps the last time through the piece, instead of every time through the second part.

</td></tr>
</table>

- Merch Megan or Megan's Daughter is a harp piece from Wales. Like Tune #8, this piece is great for working on pinches and brushes (see Exercise 38) and alternating right hand fingers while fingerpicking (see Exercises 39-45).

- The chords at the beginning of each of the first eight measures of the second part are notated for pinches using the middle, index and thumb. You can then alternate index and middle to play the rest of the fingerpicked notes in the measure. If you choose to brush these beginning chords, try alternating index and middle brushes along with alternating index and middle on the other notes.

- This version of the Irish jig, The Munster Buttermilk, is arranged for fingerpicking. The right hand fingerings make use of the idea of alternating fingers as discussed in Section Five and demonstrated in Exercises 39-45.

- For the left hand, the ring finger generally covers the first fret, middle plays notes on fret 2 and index covers the third fret.

- The Scotch Cap, a harp piece from Scotland, was arranged with the "thumb player" in mind. The left hand fingerings make use of the thumb to play melody notes while the fingers hold down other notes in the chord.

- The dot above the first note is a staccato marking. Damp this note with the left hand right after playing it, that is, prevent it from ringing by touching the string to create a clear break between this note and the next.

- Hold bass notes and middle notes as long as possible. These held notes are marked with a tie. They keep ringing while the melody moves to help create a full sound for this piece.

- In measure 8, the last three notes before the second part begins are played with the ring finger of the left hand followed by the thumb. Keep the ring on the melody string, letting it act as a guide for the index, middle and thumb that must form the chord that starts this section. Index and middle stay in position on the bass and middle strings for the first 2_ measures of the second section.

- Reaching fret 7 at the end of the third measure of the second section may seem awkward at first, but simply slide the index, already on the bass string at fret 4, up to fret 7.

<table>
<tr>
<td>

*Helpful Hints*
*for*
*Tune #12*

</td>
<td>

- Harvest Home is a wonderful study in both flatpicking and slurs. Elements of this tune form the basis for the flatpicking patterns in Exercises 16A, B, and C.

- Left hand fingering: ring finger on the first fret, middle on the second fret, index on the third fret for all three strings throughout this piece.

- Right Hand: try to alternate direction with the pick, changing direction for each note. I have notated pick direction in the beginning of the tune to provide one possible pattern to get you started.

- There are many hammer-on and pull-off combinations in this piece. For example, measure 4 starts with a hammer-on from fret one to two followed immediately by a pull-off back to fret one. This gives you three notes with one stroke of the pick. To practice these types of hammer-pull combinations refer back to Exercise 32C and D.

- Harvest Home is usually played as a hornpipe. Although I have notated the rhythm "straight" (using sequences of eighth notes) it should be played with a lilt, similar to other Irish hornpipes. Typically, the first and third eighth notes in a group of four are held a little longer with the second and fourth becoming slightly shorter. It is almost, but not quite, like playing a dotted eighth followed by a sixteenth.

</td>
</tr>
<tr>
<td>

*Helpful Hints*
*for*
*Tune #13*

</td>
<td>

- This version of the Ash Grove utilizes cross-string playing in the D-A-D-D tuning. Refer to Exercises 60-62 to explore this technique. Leave fingers in place and lets notes sustain as much as possible, especially when crossing between the two melody strings.

</td>
</tr>
<tr>
<td>

*Helpful Hints*
*for*
*Tune #14*

</td>
<td>

- This is a relatively easy five-string arrangement of The South Wind. In measures 17-20 (in the second part) the middle finger is the guide finger. It stays on the fourth string throughout. Use it to help guide the other fingers into position.

</td>
</tr>
<tr>
<td>

*Helpful Hints*
*for*
*Tune #15*

</td>
<td>

- Grace Nugent was composed by the Irish harper Turlough O'Carolan. This is a more challenging five-string arrangement that takes full advantage of the range of the instrument. The variation illustrates a small melodic variation plus an alternate way of fingering this entire passage using the thumb. In measure 13, the ring finger barre at fret 6 could also be done using ring, middle and index with the thumb playing the melody notes on the bass string that follow.

</td>
</tr>
</table>

# END NOTES

i    These ideas come from Hector Quine's Guitar Technique, pp 4-5.

ii    Quine, p 1.

iii    See Bruser, The Art of Practicing, pp 73-87.

iv    Exercises 3A, 3C, and 3D were developed by Leo Kretzner. Used with permission.

v    This method of finding a useful left hand position was suggested to me by Leo Kretzner.

vi    The basic idea of the right and left hands as artist and artisan comes from Quine, p 42.

vii    This exercise was developed by Leo Kretzner.

viii    Exercise 14A was developed by Leo Kretzner

ix    See Bruser, p. 143.

x    These exercises adapted from ideas in Guitar Fitness by Josquin De Pres

xi    Quine, p. 65

xii    This exercise was developed by Leo Kretzner.

xiii    This discussion comes partly from Quine, pp. 16-17.

# FURTHER RESOURCES

Bruser, Madeline. The Art of Practicing. A Guide to Making Music from the Heart. New York: Bell Tower, 1997.

De Pres, Josquin. Guitar Fitness. Milwaukee: Hal Leonard Publishing Corporation, 1992.

Green, Barry. The Inner Game of Music. New York: Doubleday, 1986.

Quine, Hector. Guitar Technique. Oxford: Oxford University Press, 1990.

# ABOUT THE AUTHOR

Mike Casey first placed a dulcimer on his lap in the summer of 1980, borrowing a homemade instrument that was hanging in the living room of a friend. Having just completed two years of classical guitar lessons while attending college, he immediately began playing melodies and chords over the entire instrument. Mike's interest in exploring the development of right and left hand technique on the dulcimer was inspired early on by both his classical guitar instructors and by Leo Kretzner, a fellow dulcimer player who developed exercises for the instrument in the 1980s.

Known as an innovator on the dulcimer, Mike's unique style incorporates techniques from a variety of both Irish and American instruments including banjo, mandolin, cittern, fiddle and flute, enabling him to play both melodically and stylistically with these instruments. According to Victory Review, he "takes the Appalachian dulcimer to new heights...picking the melody as intricately as a classical guitarist." Mike plays a 5-string dulcimer that has two added bass strings, giving the instrument a range that extends an octave lower than most 3-string dulcimers. He is also an accomplished Irish flute player, having journeyed to Ireland to learn from older players in the East Galway region of the country.

Mike has released two solo recordings, *The Hourglass* and *The Pleasures of Hope*, as well as two CDs with the band Cucanandy titled *He Didn't Dance* and *Contented Minds*. His music has also appeared on both volumes of the compilation CD *Masters of the Mountain Dulcimer* along with the Mel Bay collection *Dulcimer 2000*. He has taught many times at the week-long dulcimer workshop at Appalachian State University in Boone, NC; the Swannanoa Gathering at Warren Wilson College in NC; the Augusta Heritage Center in West Virginia; the Ozark Folk Center in Arkansas; Memphis Dulcimer Festival; Foothills Dulcimer Festival in Georgia, among many others. With Cucanandy he has performed at major concert venues and festivals across the country. Mike's book of Celtic repertoire for the dulcimer is forthcoming from Mel Bay. He can be reached at www.mike-casey.com.

Made in the USA
Las Vegas, NV
07 June 2022

49912059R00103